MW00937048

START WITH THIS

A Road Map for Developing Inner Strength, Vision and Work Ethic

DEANNA MCBREARTY

www.deannamcbrearty.com

Copyright © 2018 by Deanna McBrearty

All rights reserved.

No part of this book may be reproduced in any form or by any electronic or mechanical means, including information storage and retrieval systems, without written permission from the author, except for the use of brief quotations in a book review.

These are my memories, and while they may be imperfect, they are to the best of my knowledge a small collection of personal experiences while a dancer at New York City Ballet.

ISBN: 978-1-9829201-6-6

Front Cover Image courtesy of Steve Vaccariello, www.Vaccariello.com

Back Cover courtesy of Rodney Smith, www.RodneySmith.com

Editing and Formatting: Kristen Forbes, www.DeviancePress.com

Cover Art and Design: Trevor Curtis

CONTENTS

ACKNOWLEDGEMENTS

I want to thank some very special and supportive people that have been with me throughout my career and life who taught me to achieve all I can with both the opportunities and challenges I am given. I enthusiastically took advantage of every word and action you all have provided me to finish stronger. I couldn't have done it without you all.

My mom, Helen Ruth, who is the inspiration behind everything I do. From when she first said, "Start with this," and handed me a cup to help me achieve my goal of catching tadpoles, to taking me to my first ballet performance, researching the best opportunities for training, allowing me to move away from home at 13 to get more advanced training, staying with me in non air conditioned, cockroach-infested apartments (because it was all we could afford at the time) in NYC for five weeks so I could attend the prestigious School of American Ballet official summer courses, and called me at 9 p.m. on the nose every night once I moved to NYC by myself at age 16, just to make sure I was safe. Her support is tireless and endless.

My dad, Jack, for always leaving me notes of affirmation and humor under my pillow. These notes motivated me and gave me a special sense of self.

My late grandparents for their belief in my dreams and my siblings for their sacrifice (they had to move schools so I could continue my training). John, I'm still kicking my way to the top like you always encouraged me to. Helen and my brother-in-law, Derek, thank you for giving me strength and determination. I'm so inspired by all you have created as well —when are you gonna write a book about it?

My amazing, tall, dark, handsome, and blue-eyed husband, Steve Parker Jr. He pours his heart into our family daily.

Thank you for always supporting my dreams without any reservation.

My sweet, curious, and creative munchkins, Isla and Cohen. You both give me a reason to continue to challenge myself and create in this world. I can't wait to see the dreams you both make come true. Remember to always, always, always know your own truths!

My Uncle, Paul Tomasick, who gave my parents $2,000 in an envelope: the cost to send me to SAB for the summer. We couldn't afford it and neither could he, so I am forever grateful for his belief in me and that major gift - it means so much to me still.

Mr. Bertram Mandell who randomly observed class at SAB one day and chose to give a scholarship to a dedicated ballerina in training on behalf of his late wife, Maria, an Irish dancer. That was truly my lucky day!

Mr. And Mrs. Marshall Thomas, my gracious host family, for a year, when I moved away from home at age 13 to Carlisle, PA to study at Central Pennsylvania Youth Ballet. They poured their faith and love into me.

All artists that have been an influence on me that I touch upon throughout this book. Richard Corman, Steve Vaccariello, Ira Lerner, Paul Kolnik, Geoffrey Beene, Andrew Eccles, Rodney Smith, George Carlson and Wynton Marsalis.

All my teachers along the way that have blessed me under their ballet instruction especially including Suki Schorer who has been a friend, mentor and inspiration. Also Garielle

Whittle, Susan Pilarre, Kay Mazzo, Susan Stroman, Jerome Robbins, Peter Martins, Marcia Dale Weary, Melinda Howe, Re Rabassi-Davis, Phyllis Colombo, and Miss Margaret Troll. Thank you all so much.

And of course you, yes you reading this.

I want to thank you for reading *Start With This*. I hope you find inspiration and meaning in the stories and words I share. I would love to believe that I was able to pass down experiences that influence others to believe in themselves, overcome the storms of life, and leap towards and beyond their dreams.

I'd love to hear from you. Please send me a message on Instagram @DeannaMcBrearty or email me at dmc@deannamcbrearty.com.

INTRODUCTION

Start With This is the first book to dust off the myths of the dance world and take on what it really means to be an artist onstage and off. Based on the author's 12 years of experience as a renowned ballerina with the New York City Ballet, this book will give every aspiring dancer or artist at heart the insight they seek.

As thousands of young hopefuls put their toes and their dreams to the test each year, only five will be chosen by the prestigious New York City Ballet. Though the audience attendee believes each evening is pure magic, the dancer knows that behind each magic trick, there are many secrets. Behind hard work, there are sacrifices. Behind hopes, there are disappointments, and thus behind all fantasy, there is a bit of reality.

PREFACE

Ballet was my comfort zone. The place I felt the most like my true self. I could express myself, feel original, get lost in the music, set a daily challenge, stretch beyond my knowledge of my abilities, give selflessly on stage, escape to another realm, and bring the audience with me. I could learn and surprise myself daily, while maintaining the core of who I am.

In this book I share with you the joys of my highlights and the struggles of my challenges. When you're living your passion you will always face ups and downs. It's how you face the challenges and succeed that further defines your identity as a person. Sometimes it requires big leaps of faith to accomplish what we set out to do.

I've included Spotlight lessons at the end of each chapter —moments to reflect on what really matters in all of life's lessons. How can we as artists utilize any given situation, good or bad, to step in a more positive direction? To clarify our goals? To gain confidence and strengthen our talents?

Start With This does just that—it offers young adults a road map for developing inner strength, vision, and work ethic in any craft they pursue.

In the book, I share the many roles I've played in life:

- Model for designer Geoffrey Beene, gracing two of his book covers, *Geoffrey Beene; Thirty Years of Fashion* (1998) and *Beene By Beene* (Vendome Press, 2005)
- Spokesperson and model for Danskin Dancewear
- Choreographer for Barbie Dance-A-Long videos for Mattel
- Writer for *Dance Magazine*, *Dance Spirit*, and *Pointe*, and member of the advisory board at *Lifestyle Magazine*
- Film dancer in both *New York City Ballet Workouts* and several movies, including Columbia Pictures' *Center Stage*; as well as television credits include appearances on *Letterman, OWN, Good Morning America, and PBS*
- Creator of the dance-inspired workout *Balocity*

The Author's Platform

The author has extensive media experience and is a well-known dancer, lecturer, teacher, trainer, and expert in her field.

Deanna travels nationally and internationally to dance schools and arts institutes to teach, perform, and lecture. She has become a prominent, inspirational advisor to young dance students.

FOREWORD BY KURT FROMAN

Start With This is a compelling story and useful guide for any aspiring dancer, artist, or any person that wants to achieve their dream in the most proactive way possible. Drawing from her own detailed diaries, my New York City Ballet colleague has painted an extremely accurate picture of what it is like to balance a childhood with a serious commitment towards learning her craft, as well as the many struggles that happen when you have risen to the top of your field.

As a colleague at the NYCB, Deanna always stood out to me for not only her unique talent and beauty, but also her tenacity and strong will to find her own power in the dance world, which tends to be run as an autocracy. I was always amazed at Deanna's energy to seek out opportunities in the fashion and film world, something that was against the norm at our time in the Company together.

In the years since retiring from her performing career, Deanna has forged her own path and continued to spearhead her own opportunities. She has crafted a book that gleans lessons from her unique experiences growing up and is a priceless tool for any aspiring performer. I wish that I had the information and perspective she gives in the book while I was dancing in the NYCB. I have been lucky enough to work in the Broadway, TV and film world since my time as a ballet dancer, and I have used many of Deanna's ideals as a way to forge my own path going into business for myself instead of relying on life to necessarily hand me opportunities.

Hard work, talent, and ambition can take you very far, but sometimes creating opportunities that aren't even on the "game board" become the most honest and fully earned rewards. Deanna's book tells you how to get there in a way that is exciting, empowering, and thought provoking.

Kurt Froman

Kurt has worked as a Celebrity Dance Coach for Jennifer Lawrence ("Red Sparrow"), Natalie Portman and Mila Kunis ("Black Swan"), Christina Ricci (Amazon's "Z: The Beginning of Everything"), and Rooney Mara ("Song To Song"). He is a former member of the New York City Ballet, a resident choreographer for "Billy Elliot, The Musical" (Broadway and 2nd National Tour), the Original Dance Captain for Broadway's "An American in Paris," and holds the leading role in Twyla Tharp and Billy Joel's "Movin' Out" on Broadway.

FOREWORD BY SUKI SCHORER

I am very happy that Deanna McBrearty has written this book for young dancers and others who aim to succeed in a career and in life. I hope her very personal, very candid, lively, enjoyable account of her experiences as a ballet student and then as a member of the New York City Ballet reaches a wide public.

Ballet entertains the audience by creating an illusion of ease. Nothing looks difficult, tiring, painful. As dancers take their bows, the audience typically sees smiling faces, refined behavior, relaxed graciousness. In fact, for the people on stage, it's not always that way. Dancers make sure the audience is aware of none of what ballet actually requires.

Deanna's many anecdotes of her life as a dancer ring completely true to me. They remind me of my own years preparing for a career, then dancing professionally. Dancing always took a lot, both physically and mentally and teaching still does. It has been everything I dreamt of as a girl, and more. I have fully enjoyed my work and have been and still am completely committed, as I had to be and still must be.

I remember so clearly Deanna's unfailing positive spirit,

the joy in dancing, the hard work in class and rehearsal, and the many beautiful performances I saw. All that came from her determination to achieve, to turn both favorable and unfavorable moments into building blocks for better results next time. Hard times, all times, were used to re-think and adjust. Nothing was wasted. I hope her readers are able to take inspiration from her example.

Suki Schorer

Suki is a former NYCB principal dancer, a Dance Magazine Award recipient, Author of Suki Schorer on Balanchine Technique, and a Brown Foundation Senior Faculty Chair at School of American Ballet.

NEVER GIVE UP ON YOUR DREAMS

 Your talent is there for a reason. Use it and it
will define your greatest dream."
    - Isla Parker, nine years old

It all started when I was old enough to dream bigger than my hometown. Hazleton, Pennsylvania had beautiful mountains and kind, hard-working people, but the best opportunities are not always in the town you are born. You have to seek them. In all cases of extreme self-advancement, you must go where the challenge lies. Your reality becomes what you allow it to be. My hometown was limited in its offerings, and my desire to achieve made me willing to travel anywhere to find *more*.

When I was 10 years old, I went to see the Pennsylvania Ballet perform *The Nutcracker* while visiting my cousins at Christmas. I had never seen anything like it—Tchaikovsky's beautiful music, the colorful costumes, the exciting choreography. It transported me to a grand new world, one I immediately wanted to be a part of.

Fortunately, I didn't have to beg my mother to take ballet

lessons. Her own dance training had been cut short as a child, when she had lost her mother at only 14 years old. But she had never lost a love for dance, so she sent me to my first class with the only teacher in town, Ms. Troll.

Skinny and wrinkly with her grey hair always up in a bun, Ms. Troll gave me lessons on the carpet in her living room. The back of an armchair served as a makeshift barre. She was strict but she taught me the basics of ballet: vocabulary, how to memorize combinations, how to hear and move with music.

Before discovering dance, I wasn't very confident. In class, I found a place where my long neck and bony arms could be used to accentuate my movements. My "bird legs,"as my sister used to call them, could take me across the floor. Ms. Troll recognized that I learned quickly and had a natural ability to move, so she encouraged me to dedicate myself. And I did.

After a few short months, she decided I was ready for Capezio Pavlowa pointe shoes. My feet were smaller than the smallest size carried, so she had to special order them straight from the factory. I waited quite impatiently for them to arrive, bugging my mom each afternoon to see if she'd received them. We couldn't even afford them, so she saved them to present to me as a Christmas present.

The first time I put them on, I was afraid of scuffing the pretty pink satin: I wanted to keep them nice-looking forever! I stuffed the inside with lamb's wool until it overflowed in clumps, thinking more about comfort than technique. With my new pointe shoes, I learned a dance routine that involved cartwheels and a baton, to a song that repeated the phrase "Tick-Tock."

My first ever pair of pointe shoes. This is what living room training looks like.

Since Ms. Troll's studio didn't stage productions often, and I pretty much slept in my pointe shoes, my mom dedicated her free time to taking me to all the assisted living homes in town so I could show off my talents and get a taste of performing. I was a big hit with the residents wherever I went. They met my leaps and pointe work with "oohs" and "ahhs." When my eyes met their smiling faces, I realized how much I loved being able to express myself creatively while making others feel good.

Just one year after seeing *The Nutcracker*, I'd found my outlet: it had something to do with body language, and ballet would be my voice. I wanted more applause, but I knew nothing about technique. If I wanted to be serious about ballet and have more opportunities to perform, then I needed more of a challenge to take my talents to the next level.

I convinced my mom to take me to "real" ballet classes at a "real" ballet school in Wilkes-Barre, a town 45minutes away. Wilkes-Barre Ballet Theater had two large studios with black Marley floors and a real, double-height barre. The school offered one class a day for my level and a series of performances at the end of the year. I knew I had to take advantage of both.

My first "real" Ballet class at Wilkes-Barre Ballet Theater.
The pink hair ribbon helped me look official.

If I started taking lessons there, my mom would have to drive me after school every day. I was the youngest of three, so this wasn't a simple task. Yet somehow, she knew that ballet was for me, so she supported my dream and agreed to swap the carpool with my dad.

One of them would pick me up immediately after the school bell rang every afternoon. I would eat dinner and do my homework in the car in order to arrive at the studio with enough time to change into a leotard and tights, fix my long hair into a bun, and stretch before class began. I loved every second of it.

One day after class, I noticed a sign posted on the board:

Looking for Young Ballet Dancers
Ages 12 - 14, no taller than 4'10"
Take part in a five-week training program for a one-time performance with New York City Ballet in Saratoga Springs

I was 12 years old and four feet, eight inches tall, so I thought this flier was asking for me personally. I knew nothing about the New York City Ballet, but I knew enough about New York City from trips with my family to know that if you could make it there, you could make it anywhere. My mind was made up: this was my chance for the big leagues. I just *had* to go to Saratoga Springs.

My mom's mind, on the other hand, was on the five-hour car ride to get there. Luckily, all it took was a bit of convincing for four of my dance friends and their parents to carpool. Soon enough, I'd be on my way.

On the morning we left for Saratoga Springs at 4 a.m., it was dark and chilly. My dad had loaded the backbench seat of our Bonneville with warm blankets, fluffy pillows, and Goldfish crackers in preparation for the long ride ahead. I was too excited to sleep. Midway, I hopped into another car with all my friends so we could chatter excitedly about what we thought would happen at the audition.

When we finally got there, I knew deep in my heart that this day would mark my first step to becoming a professional ballet dancer. When my friends and I checked in, we were given audition numbers to pin to our leotards. In groups of 20 dancers, we entered the audition studio. There were teachers observing and a costume-fitting crew waiting to take measurements. There inside the studio, we learned a 16-count combination of choreography that we were then asked to perform, moving from the back of the room to the front.

Showing nerves before the audition for a chance to perform with NYCB in Saratoga Springs, NY.

When it was my turn, I felt so happy as I pas de basqued my way forward. They gently reminded us to smile, to gauge who had stage presence. I couldn't have smiled any bigger. I was in my element. I may not have known as many technical steps as the other girls did, but I knew how to emulate the instructor.

When the first part of the audition ended, I came out crying. My mom ran to me and started trying to soothe me with heartfelt support. "It's your first audition," she consoled, patting my back. "Things don't happen overnight."

But I was crying because I couldn't believe I'd made the first cut. I'd wanted it so badly, and all of my hard work had paid off!

To my mom's relief, I made the second cut too. I was chosen to perform in Jerome Robbins' ballet *Circus Polka* on stage with the New York City Ballet. It was a dream come true! I'd get to spend five weeks learning the piece in preparation for their summer season at the Saratoga Performing Arts Center.

———

Those five weeks were an introduction to ballet beyond my imagination or what I'd seen in my hometown. The Saratoga Performing Arts Center was an outdoor theater and rehearsal space. The main studio, where all the company dancers trained, had a wall of windows. Before each of my rehearsals, the company members would warm up with a class conducted in the main studio. I arrived early each rehearsal to watch the whole company take class before each performance.

Most notably, I saw principal dancer Heather Watts rehearsing the extremely powerful and patriotic *Stars and Stripes*. Her beautiful, nonstop footwork on pointe introduced me to ways of moving I'd never seen before. I was awestruck. She was "Ballet" to me. I wanted to be just like her: not realizing, of course, all that I had to learn before I could be like Heather. I'd learn a good chunk of it that summer though, and Garielle Whittle—the ballet mistress for the children at School of American Ballet, the school affiliated with New York City Ballet—would be the one to teach me.

Garielle was responsible for grooming the dancers at School of American Ballet, the school New York Ballet typically chooses from. She was an incredible, admirably patient woman. I earned special attention from her when my part in *Circus Polka* required an advanced step that I'd never heard of before: an *entrechat quatre*. I wasn't sure how to do it, and she'd be the one to teach me.

After rehearsal, I was summoned by Garielle to lie on my back on the studio floor. To my surprise, she kneeled down and tied a leg warmer around my ankles. As she helped me to my feet, she explained how to properly do the jump: "While keeping your legs together, your thighs touching, and your ankles crossed, beat your feet front-to-back, front-to-back. The leg warmer tied around your ankles will force your beats to be tight and fast. This is your homework."

Garielle Whittle correcting my form in rehearsal for Jerome Robbins' "Circus Polka." Saratoga Springs, NY.

Every night for the next five weeks, I practiced with the leg warmer. One beat at a time, I learned discipline, dedication to detail, and the art of perfection. And with each day, I learned to have patience through long hours of rehearsals. The performances were just as much fun backstage—with all my new dance friends—as it was on stage. I had managed to master all my steps and never lost my smile, even with all the concentration required.

The final gala was as much a production for the audience as for the dancers on stage. The theater grounds were covered with circus-themed pre-performance events, including jugglers, magician acts, elephant rides, and free popcorn! By the end of that summer, I knew how to focus on my dream. I'd gained a clearer vision of what I wanted and what was possible, which would fuel me to work harder than ever.

In Saratoga, I heard about the School of American Ballet's renowned summer program in New York City, and I knew where I wanted to be the following year. This program was different. It concentrated on class training for focused dancers to sharpen their skills, and not just on preparation for a production. I'd learned that there would be an audition process in several months and only 100 dancers from across the world would be chosen to train in New York for the summer. I wanted to be ready.

When I returned home, I continued training at Wilkes-Barre, leaving junior high every afternoon to fit in a 90-minute ballet class every night. No more football games or late-night tag. No more parties or hanging out with friends after school. My only friends were other ballet dancers.

Dancers from Wilkes-Barre Ballet Theater strike a pose for the local paper.
That's me in Sos-sous.

I worked hard for five grueling months, auditioned in January, and waited a painstaking month to receive my acceptance by mail. There was no question in my mind that dancing was what I wanted to do.

———

A year after leaving New York, I returned to take my place with dancers from all over the world. Over the next five weeks, I did nothing but dance. I had a 90-minute ballet class every morning, and my afternoons were filled with character, pointe, and variations classes, where we learned actual Balanchine choreography. I liked to arrive a half hour early before each class to stretch and get my head in the game, erasing any outside thoughts or cares. All that mattered was ballet.

Me taking notes from Suzanne Farrell, one of Balanchine's most celebrated muses, prior to SAB workshop performance.

Each morning, Associate Director Madame Gleboff took attendance and observed the first few minutes of each class. The teachers would whisper things to her, making observations about us. I couldn't mess up when they focused their attention my way! I did my best not to get distracted and worked as hard as I could every class. I wanted so eagerly to impress my teachers: Suki Schorer, Susan Pilarre, Antonina Tumkovsky, and Andrei Kramarevsky. Whenever they gave me corrections during class, I wrote them down to reread and absorb that night.

Me and the beloved Antonina Tumkovsky in a studio at School of American Ballet during my first summer course. She taught generations of NYCB dancers for 54 years. Her classes were demanding and crucial for stamina.

Me and Suki Schorer, a Balanchine ballerina and my mentor and teacher at SAB. Her classes were so musical. She has dedicated her entire career to Balanchine aesthetics and technique.

By the end of the five-week summer course, the faculty

created an evaluation for every dancer, and Madame Gleboff would be the bearer. During our last week, appointments were made for the dreaded office visits. Madame Gleboff was known for being straight-faced and telling dancers boldly whether they had potential or not. As I waited out in the hallway for my appointment, I watched other girls come out of the office either crying, sweating, or shrugging with mild relief. Occasionally, a girl would half-skip down the hall —she'd been asked to stay for the year-round program.

Even before I entered her office, I knew from my instructors' corrections over the summer that I had a lot of work to do. My evaluation was just what I needed to hear to direct my confidence and assure me that I was on the right track: "You are a hard worker and the teachers like you. You are welcome back next summer, provided you keep up the good work." I intended to!

After the summer course, I went back to my classes at Wilkes-Barre. Eventually I realized I was no longer being challenged at that school and needed to move on if I was serious about dancing.

My mom was there to guide me. She taught me that you can always make things happen for yourself. When it came to my brother, my sister, and me, she believed in anything we wanted to accomplish, even if that goal was to catch every tadpole in Lake Wallenpaupack. She would hand us a plastic cup and say, "Start with this."

You have to start somewhere, and it helps to have someone who believes in you and can help guide you. Even if that mentor is not a parent, it can be sought in a teacher or even deep within yourself. Whatever support you find should give you the strength to be unafraid to go for anything. For me, I found that support in my parents, and they helped me take the next step toward my dream.

They scouted a more serious ballet school in Carlisle, PA,

called Central Pennsylvania Youth Ballet. CPYB was a two-hour drive from our home in Hazleton, and we made that drive to visit the school together. My mom and I observed classes and concluded that it was exactly what I needed. The next step would be to register me in the school system and find a host family to house me. My mom decided it would be best to do a trial investment.

I would finish my last few months of eighth grade in the Carlisle school district, keeping the same schedule of fitting in academics until 2 p.m. in order to leave early and study ballet. If I wasn't happy by the end of the summer, then only three months would have been lost rather than an entire year.

There wasn't really a decision to be made on my part. I wasn't nervous about leaving my friends that I had known since kindergarten; I was looking forward to meeting new ones. I wasn't afraid to leave home or be on my own; I was excited to learn and looked forward to the move like it were a long, extended vacation.

———

Two weeks before I was scheduled to move, there came a bump in the road. In a routine exam at my junior high, the school nurse noticed something suspicious in the way my back was shaped when I bent over to touch my toes. She told me to make an appointment with a specialist at a nearby hospital.

After some x-rays, I was diagnosed with a serious case of scoliosis. My spine was curved in an S shape, and it would only get worse if I didn't do something to correct it immediately. I was two degrees of curve away from requiring surgery, so I was told I'd have to wear a brace, which would stiffen my back and leave me with no flexibility. And, the doctor explained, it wouldn't even correct the curve: it would just keep it from getting worse.

"No one heals from this kind of curvature," he explained. "You won't have any flexibility for sports, let alone dance. You will not be able to dance with a back like this."

I had too many questions and twisted emotions buzzing around in my head to appear strong any longer. My face became a pool of tears. No one had ever let me in on such a harsh truth: I wouldn't fulfill my dreams.

I had nothing further to say to that doctor. I took the specially-molded, plastic body brace they gave me that day and strapped it around my midsection, feeling alien and crooked. I left the hospital in my "improved" stance, angry but determined. I may have been broken on the outside but I was unwavering on the inside. I would wear that brace 24 hours a day until my skin peeled off, if that's what it took to go to CPYB.

But all of the stress wore at me. Days later, I came down with a 104-degree fever and had to miss my last few days of junior high. Even then, I still refused to take the brace off. My parents were worried and my mom was afraid that all of this was some kind of sign that I shouldn't move forward with my plan. In my mind, there was no turning back. I was not going to give up on my dream. So I left for CPYB as scheduled, one week before my 14th birthday.

I moved in with my host family, the Thomas's, an older couple in their 60s. I loved my new situation. I finally had my own room, which made me feel "adult" and responsible as I organized "my life." Mrs. Thomas was a fabulous cook and Mr. Thomas loved to act silly with me. And every second that I wasn't dancing, I wore that back brace, even while I slept.

Me with my host family, The Thomas's.

Mr. Thomas took on the responsibility of driving me to school and dance. In the afternoon, we had an hour to spare for lunch between school and ballet, and he'd often take me to his dental lab, where he made false teeth for a living. He'd encourage me to take a break from my itchy, sweaty back brace in those moments. The straps were complicated and located on the back where I could not easily manage alone. I'd remove it and we'd pray together for my spine to be healed. I truly believed that I would be.

One month later, I saw the same doctor for a checkup. He moved his fingers along my spine and didn't speak, then sent me immediately for x-rays. After he'd received the results, he came into my examination room with a puzzled look on his face.

"What have you been doing?" he asked. "Your spine is absolutely straight!" He seemed shocked, attempting to explain once again that a back brace can only prevent a spine for curving further, and how it can take up to three months to show any results.

I believed in miracles from then on, but mostly I learned not to give up on my dreams.

SPOTLIGHT LESSON

Only you can put limits on yourself, so what would you picture if the sky were the limit? What is your dream? What if you started to ask, "Why not me? Why couldn't the things I want happen to me?" And what if you started to believe it?

1. **Write down what you dream for yourself.** Make a list of things you want to see or accomplish. Don't let anyone else's words or opinions seep in. Don't listen to the voice that tells you that you can't have those things. A lot can be accomplished with faith.
2. **Picture making those dreams come true.** Every night before you fall asleep, visualize yourself in the place you want to be.

Notes:

LEARN TO WORK HARD

 The best way to be is to do. Thought is creative; word is productive; action is divine."
- Wynton Marsalis

As a new student, I was not a star. Marcia Dale Weary, the founder of CPYB, was reluctant to take me on initially, because not only did I wear my back brace to improve scoliosis, but I'd started wearing an elastic support knee brace from previous growing pain injuries. She saw that there was a weakness in me and knew that the workload on her students was strenuous, so she questioned my physical capabilities. My family couldn't even afford CPYB, but Marcia still took a chance on me. I was going to have to work hard to prove I was worth it.

My first week at the Barn—literally an old barn converted into dance studios—was grueling. It was hard to imagine that anything other than sheep were going to walk through the door when I opened it for the first time. But the image of Marcia herding sheep out of a barn upon purchase in 1957 to replace them with barres and mirrors is a testament to her insight and devotion—the same traits she expected to instill in her dancers.

I would arrive after school, around 2 p.m., to clean bathrooms as part of my partial scholarship. I would replace toilet paper, wipe down the counters, and make sure there was enough country flower-scented air freshener in each.

Me and Marcia Dale Weary at Central Pennsylvania Youth Ballet studios.

Once I was done, I'd attend my first class of the afternoon for an hour. It was held in the smaller studio that was rectangular in shape, which meant I was closer to my image in the mirror when I held onto the barre. I could see every placement nuance in my reflection that I had not yet learned to perfect, including my "chicken wing" arms: it seemed I couldn't keep from dropping my elbows and bending my wrists. Maybe I was channeling the farm animal predecessors.

Between my first and second classes, I'd wipe handprints off the mirrors in all three studios and vacuum the thinning carpet in the waiting room where the other dancers used to eat, leaving behind their crumbs. Then I'd dance for another several hours of classes in studio classes with hardwood floors, wood-paneled walls, and floor fans for air conditioning. In between each class, I'd go back to check and clean the bathrooms, vacuum, and wipe the mirrors. And so it went between each of my 21 ballet classes per week.

I eventually started to settle into my new life in Carlisle. Monday through Friday, I went to my academic classes until 1 p.m., but skipped out on lunch period, study hall, and gym. Then I'd get a ride to the Barn from my host family to dance until 9 p.m. each day, including Saturdays. Back in Hazleton, I'd seen my dad leave our warm house at 3 a.m. on icy mornings to fix downed electrical lines after a storm, as part of his job at Pennsylvania Power and Light. Watching him go out into the freezing weather was my introduction to what it meant to work hard.

At 14 years old, I had a long way to go to strengthen my technique. Marcia placed me in classes with 9-year-olds who already had years of experience beyond me. I watched them dance with boys in partnering classes, do fouette turns on pointe, and perform a repertoire of complex Balanchine choreography—all things I'd never done before.

Everyone got corrections in classes, but mine seemed to be the same ones over and over again. Melinda, one of my teachers, would tell me to straighten my knees fully, to lengthen my arched back, to hold my elbows up higher, and use my plié more. I was constantly faced with the reality of how far behind the other talent I was.

There is a saying that goes "it's about quality, not quantity," but at CPYB our training was about adding quality to quantity. My teachers insisted that we put in a level of quality beyond our present abilities. Our dedication was expected to show through in the level of detail and thought we gave to every movement we made. Our techniques were broken down to a painstakingly slow process so we could truly comprehend and emphasize correctness in every movement.

Standing in front of a mirror, we would practice the way we carried our arms by starting with our back muscles, then connecting our shoulders, our elbows, and our wrists—in that order. We would work through the mechanics of fouette turns by going through each position slowly and repeatedly: passé, extend the working leg to the front while bending the leg we stood on, carry the working leg to the side while deepening the plié, then pull the working leg back into a passé with no turn, just to force the upper body to be involved to find the momentum needed to actually turn. We'd do this eight times slowly on each side, defining what it meant to have patience and working through quality in every detail.

I worked hard, but the results took time and relentless effort. When my class prepared to perform Balanchine's *Raymonda Variations* for a visiting Soviet dignitary, I learned each step of the several solos that make up the piece. It was my first exposure to Balanchine's choreography and I loved every one of them. Still, I was cast in the corps. I watched my classmates—who were lucky enough to be chosen to perform the solos—from the back of the room. It was hard not to feel frustrated. I knew I had potential but was not quite skilled enough.

Somehow all of the corrections and the disappointment of being behind just became an impetus to work even harder. I knew I had so much to learn. If I could just focus on the end goal of becoming a ballerina one day, then the present moment of being an awkward duckling wouldn't seem so permanent. So, I analyzed my movements to the tiniest detail, and made sure to absorb and take tediously hand-written notes on all my corrections.

I stuck to Marcia's strict policies on appearance. She believed it helped you live the part you were trying to become. I learned to dress the part of a professional ballerina by pulling my hair back tightly into a bun and using purple Aqua Net aerosol hairspray to prevent any "whispies," or baby hairs blowing in the wind. I used a small amount of pale, pink blush on my cheeks, placed rhinestone earrings in my ears, and pinned a red flower into my bun.

I never swayed from that dress code, even years later when I left to attend School of American Ballet in New York

City. Dressing the part of what I wanted to become gave me the confidence to embody the quality I would eventually achieve. I continued to wear Marcia's traditional uniform of black leotard and pink tights, a flower in my hair, and rhinestone earrings. To this day, Marcia's students can be recognized anywhere because of the image she instills of what a classical ballerina should look like.

She also thought of many ways to build our work ethic. Her methods not only increased our physical strength but our mental dedication too. We had to work hard in class and show progress to earn the right to sew ribbons on our ballet slippers or wear a colored leotard. We could be "hired" to teach our peers for $1 per class. It was never about earning money, but about training our eyes to critique and then correct our fellow students. In turn, we'd be able to recognize what needed to be corrected in ourselves as we danced in front of the mirror.

This methodical system worked on me. I took every opportunity I was given to learn and work as hard and as much as I could. Outside of my scheduled regimen of classes, I asked Marcia if I could sit in on rehearsals that I wasn't even cast for, just to be able to learn more. I volunteered to be a part of lecture demonstrations at the local college to have more performance opportunities. Marcia always said that we needed to do more than what was expected of us to surpass our current level of talent. I believed her and I gave it everything I had.

One Sunday afternoon, my only day off after a long week of classes and rehearsals, I sat in my room wanting to rest. I knew there was an optional hour-and-a-half class that Marcia taught at another studio, and I thought about going. I wondered if I had the energy to add more hours of training onto the ones I'd already worked through during the week.

Was it even worth it since I was always the student to get

corrected nonstop anyway? Was it worth it since I was overlooked for lead parts in all of our shows? Was it worth it because I was older than the 9-year-olds who were doing double fouette turns on point like smooth, spinning tops, while I was just figuring out how to keep from getting cross-eyed through one turn? I decided it was and hitched a ride with Marcia.

We rode in comfortable silence for about 15 minutes before Marcia said, "Deanna, you will succeed faster than the other students. I see your commitment. You came in with less but you will leave with more because you are focused. I see your progress. When you give effort, it pays off. You will soon surpass those who have been here since they were eight.   I enjoy your company on Sundays and your commitment."

That small remark gave me more gumption to work and justified my previous effort. Those words made me confident my exhausting efforts would one day lead me to somewhere special. I was at CPYB—far away from home, my childhood friends, and my family—trying to focus on something I only knew as a passion. There were no guarantees and no previous maps to follow that would help me measure each step along the way. Up to this point, everything I did was based on passion. But that day in the car, Marcia's encouragement made me realize that it's one thing to have passion for what you do, it's a whole other level to apply focus and effort too.

SPOTLIGHT LESSON

Do you know where your comfort zone is? Do you know what it feels like to move beyond that place? Do you know how to challenge yourself to do things that don't come easily for you? If you want to learn to work hard, start by opening up to the opportunities around you.

1. **Try saying "yes" to everything.** Accept an invitation. Take an extra class. Sign up for an extracurricular activity that interests you. Volunteer at a soup kitchen. Help someone when they ask. If you are willing to participate and try new things, you will learn to do more than you thought you could.

2. **Practice going the extra mile.** Where can you get more involved? If one thing is requested or expected of you, do that and then do one more thing. That's where discovery lies. It's your "second wind" area: the place where you learn you can do something you didn't imagine was possible. Where you're not settling—you're committing and putting yourself in a position to let others notice.

Notes:

CONTRACT INTO COMPANY

 The way I experience the world is through my art. It becomes my diary. My experience. It's the best thing I do."
- Richard Corman, on photographing athletes of the Special Olympics

I ran to the nearest payphone—down the hall from the main studio—to call my mom. "Hi mom, it's me!" I said, my voice shaking.

"What's wrong, Deanna?" she answered, with a mother's natural perception.

"I got it! I'm in! I'm officially part of the company now!" I said, the excitement bursting in chest. "They just gave me my contract!"

Each word I uttered spilled out with as much exclamation as the first. Pretty soon the conversation overflowed with so much excitement that I couldn't differentiate her words from mine. My dad was at work when I called, but I could hear in my thoughts exactly what he would say: "Slim, I knew you would kick your way to the top."

Mom of course wanted the whole story from the beginning again with all the details. "Yeah, so, I was in rehearsal for *Symphony in 3 Movements*, a ballet that I can only understudy because I already performed my five ballets for the season."

The rules of apprenticeship say you are only allowed to be cast in no more than five ballets per season for up to two years. If you are needed in a sixth ballet, they must give you your contract. There are never any guarantees though that they will ever give you that sixth ballet or your contract for that matter.

"So Rosemary, our ballet mistress arrived late to rehearsal and announced that one of the dancers will be having back surgery and will be gone for the rest of the season. She needed to replace her and asked me to stand in. I'm not even her understudy! I was learning a different part. So, I did the rehearsal, just following along, trying to retain my joy that this could mean six ballets! At the end of the rehearsal, Rosemary said to so casually, 'Oh yes, Deanna, so you know what this means, you are one of us now.' And that was it. Then I called you!"

The voice over the phone proudly exclaimed from 150 miles away in Pennsylvania, "Wow, Deanna, you made it in NYC!" I could tell she didn't want to hang up.

I had a rehearsal on stage next so I had to hang up the phone. I ran to stage for the full run-through rehearsal with the principal dancers, the cream of the crop celebrities of the dance world! Up until this time, the corps dancers had rehearsed their sections of the ballet without the main leads. A full-out rehearsal with everyone together on stage only takes place the day the ballet runs for the first time in the season.

My heart was pounding in my chest but my mind had to stay razor-sharp. Little did I realize this was foreshadowing my "crash course repertory," where I would be required to learn a ballet in a few hours—or even minutes—during the afternoon and perform it convincingly that evening.

When I arrived on stage level, Peter Martins was standing by the water fountain. He turned to me with a big Cheshire cat grin. He gave me a firm handshake that made me lose my balance and said, "Congratulations. Isn't that great news? Don't forget to sign your contract." It had been a year to date, June 6, since I joined as an apprentice, and I still felt swallowed by his presence.

Peter Martins demonstrating a partnering move on me during company class, on stage, David H. Koch Theater. New York City Ballet. Photo credit Paul Kolnik.

Rehearsal started. The opening section of the ballet

included 16 regular, corps de ballet ladies lined up in a diagonal without principals involved, so all went smoothly for me. My confidence was up because Rosemary had expressed that she was impressed with how I fit right in and learned so quickly.

In the next section of the ballet, I was in a choreographed clump with seven other corps dancers at the bottom of stage left. My back was turned away from center stage and little was I aware that a principal dancer enters at that time. Damian Woetzel was ready to have a moment of glory as he turned like a top in center stage. I should mention that Damian wasn't just any principal dancer—he was a very *cute* principal dancer. Every aspiring ballerina (and half the audience) had a crush on Damian Woetzel.

As he spun, I gracefully jogged around the corner and continued my own steps with deep, blind-to-the-world focus. Next came the time for my group to mesh with the other group flawlessly past center stage, as Damian continued to turn in center stage. As I faced the other group, I was left stunned, unsure of which side of Damian I was to cross.

Within seconds, my body decided for me, and I found myself split-legged in a straddle sit under Damian Woetzel! I pictured myself turning into a turtle and retracting into my shell, when Damian spoke...to me! "So, is this a proposal?" he asked flirtatiously.

I smiled and gave him my left hand for a ring. He pulled me by my hand and swept me off my "newly corps" butt and back onto my graceful dancer feet. *What an unexpected start*, I thought.

As Peter watched from the front of stage, he shared a pearl of wisdom, "Bad dress rehearsal means good performance." And it was true: all shows go better after a mishap-filled rehearsal because it keeps you aware and adrenaline-soaked, as opposed to complacent and assuming. That day I not only signed a contract with New York City Ballet, but I also signed one with my subconscious. That was the one and only time I would ever let myself fall on stage.

I discovered how life's surprises can lead to growth. If you can envision it, then you can convince yourself of it. If you can convince yourself of it, you can make it happen for yourself. It's all a bit tricky, but you can learn to know yourself extremely well, and to know exactly what you want to expect from yourself. It became my technique for staying strong and confident amid the stress and pressure of life in the arts.

SPOTLIGHT LESSON

Think about how you can allow growth by asking yourself how you can do things differently next time.

1. **Analyze.** Take the opportunity you have been given as a moment to mentally choose the outcome you want. Play an active role in the end result by allowing growth in every motion, even in mistakes.
2. **Stay Alert.** By being aware at all times, you will keep your actions alive, grounded, and anticipating.

Notes:

BACK TO THE BASICS

 GREAT ART is always a balancing act. But all
art has both—an emotional content and an
intellectual content."
- George Carlson

It all started like a typical day. I was 22 years old and four
years deep into the company schedule of 10 a.m. - 11 p.m.,
six days a week. One Tuesday morning, a half-hour before
ballet class started, I arrived at my dressing room spot on the
fourth floor of the David H. Koch Theater. I was wearing
fitted jazz pants because I always hated wearing restrictive
tights during the day, and they were also required for
performances at night.

Using my lucky hair band, I pulled my hair up into a bun.
I always waited until I was inside the theater to do this,
because I hated being recognized on the street as a dancer. It
was inevitable that someone would approach and remark,
"You're a dancer, aren't you? I can tell by your hair." Either
that, or "by your walk" or "by your posture".

*Backstage preparing in front of my dressing room mirror
for a performance.*

I decided to break out my stage makeup and add a little extra mascara to my eyes to make them look more awake. It was mid-*Nutcracker* season and my face showed how tired I was feeling. I took a long look at myself in the mirror and reflected on my memories of dance class as a teenager. It had required a lot of dedication and devotion on my side. My school friends would always invite me to join them in a game of tag or to hang out at a football game, and I'd always have the same response: "Sorry, I have ballet."

For me, it wasn't a problem to tell them no, that I had something I was dedicated to and wouldn't be able to join in on their fun. What was harder was when they stopped inviting me altogether because they already knew the answer. That is when I realized I was setting myself apart and involving myself in another world, so to speak. Random people would always comment on what a sacrifice it was to be a dancer and how much I had to miss, and they'd ask if it bothered me.

Deep down inside, I loved to dance. It had been hard to know I was missing out on some other fun, but because I'd been doing something I loved to do and could possibly do every day for a living, dance had never felt like a sacrifice. The minute I would hear the classical music and class started, there wasn't anywhere in the world I would rather be.

With this thought in mind, I returned to staring in the dressing room mirror and posed that very question to my 22-year-old self, *Would you rather be anywhere else?* My answer was still a loud and proud, *No.*

Class began at its usual 10:30 a.m. time, and I was feeling nice and limber from my 20-minute stretch leading up to it. It lasted an hour and a half, with a little sweat and a lot of focus. I still had a full day ahead of me. Rehearsals would start immediately after class and run from noon to 6 p.m. Union rules mandated a five-minute break every hour, and an hour break every three hours, but when my body still ached from the day before, that didn't feel like often enough.

I was scheduled to rehearse four different ballets by 6 p.m., none of which were *The Nutcracker*, the ballet I would be performing that evening. Instead, I'd be rehearsing our regular repertory ballets which were scheduled for performance two days after *The Nutcracker*'s run was over.

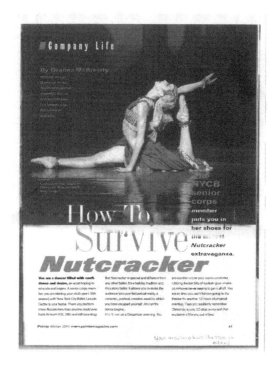

*Clipping of a fun journal article I wrote for Pointe Magazine on surviving
The Nutcracker. Photo of me in the Arabian dance in Balanchine's "The
Nutcracker," New York City Ballet. Photo credit Paul Kolnik.*

In our regular repertory season, we would perform up to
45 different ballets. Every night was a different combination
of three or four ballets. As a highly-used corps member, I
would be cast in close to 35 of the 45 ballets! It was like
having a final exam every single day. We would learn three
different ballets in three days, and perform them back-to-
back in one night. Although we would never rehearse those
ballets again, we would be expected to perform them two
more times later in the 14-week repertory season. My
memory was constantly shuffling and trying to make room
for all the memorized choreography.

After a long day of rehearsals, it was time to prepare for

my evening performance. We had from 6 to 8 p.m. to prep ourselves. During those two hours, I sewed a new pair of shoes (I typically went through a pair of pointe shoes per day). As usual, I spent 40 minutes just on my stage make-up. Before I knew it, the two hours were up, and I headed to the practice room studio on the fifth floor to warm up for the second time that day.

I ran on stage to take a bow for Marzipan. Despite it only being the start of week two and show number 15, I was tired and my body had no juice in its muscles. My typically graceful ballet run had a slight limp to it. With every weight-bearing tap of my pointe shoe on the floor, nerve pain shot up my left foot and shin. I pleaded with my thoughts that mind would prevail over matter.

For three weeks prior, my foot hadn't felt normal. I'd hoped for rest for the weary, but there was always another ballet to rehearse, or role to strive for. There was always another friend or family member who had already purchased tickets to see me perform. Sometimes, admitting to injury and pulling myself out of performing caused more mental suffering than the pain of the injury itself.

There were great things to look forward to in the upcoming rep season, including my favorite ballet, *Agon*. I hated the idea of making headway, only to take two steps back because of injury. I told myself, *I'm not injured, it's only irritated. All I need is some Advil.*

I preached this to myself until the fat lady sang! I came off stage after bows and took the pointe shoe off of my throbbing foot. Once the tight elastic loosened its grip on my circulation, my foot became that fat lady singing (and *boy* was she fat, and what a tune she was belting!). Once my eyes registered the incredible swelling—the surest sign of a problem—I knew it was all over. I had to give in. "Dancer down, I'm out."

News got out and Rosemary began the replacement domino effect: What parts was I cast for the rest of the week? What was I rehearsing for rep? Who was my understudy? Who is their understudy if they step out of their part to step into mine? What rehearsals will need to be cancelled in order to make time for emergency rehearsals?

I got into the elevator and headed for the therapy room four flights up from stage. My best friend from childhood, Michelle, was one of the physical therapists. Having studied at School of American Ballet herself, she was well aware of the dancer's body and its manipulative compensation techniques.

It was immediately obvious to her that I'd been dancing with my foot out of joint for so long that my foot had decided to lock itself in the "out" position in order to get me on stage at all. My cuboid was dropped, my talis was locked forward, and my forth metatarsil was like a fallen bridge. It may sound like pig Latin, but all dancers learn to recognize these technical terms eventually.

On a regular basis, I never spent any time in the therapy room unless it was to chit chat with Michelle. From that day forward, I would "become one" with the therapy room and all of its voodoo gels, electric zappers, and topical remedies. It would've been easier to have a break or sprain, something definable. My injury was one which required a whole lot of waiting and very little knowing. It went undiagnosed for days until the swelling went down enough for a therapist to notice my bones were out of place.

After that, it took weeks until the muscles relaxed enough in my calf and foot to allow a therapist to pop my joints back into their rightful positions. Because I had danced so long with them out of place, even once they were put back in place, the overstretched and nerve-damaged ligaments didn't want to hold and keep in position.

For months I rehabbed, observed rehearsals, and stubbornly tried to mark my rehearsals in flat ballet slippers instead of pointe shoes, but the pain never left me. I had never felt so frustrated and depressed. My foot was in total control of me, causing my dancing to lag behind. I was putting in the work without getting any results. I grew concerned as my roles were given to others. I was constantly confronted by others with unanswerable questions: When will you be back dancing? What exactly is the injury? Why can't you just tape it in place?

Dealing with injuries is very difficult for a dancer. Our art form depends on all of our joints and body parts working at their prime. When they don't cooperate, we are forced to slow down and take time off, which cultivates many fears: Will I lose all my strength? Will I ever heal again? Will I be forgotten? A dancer's jerk reaction is to rush the healing process just to get on stage, but if you don't let an injury heal properly, you risk the condition becoming chronic.

This was my one and only debilitating injury of my career, and it was an undiagnosed mystery as to how I could most speedily heal it and prevent it from resurfacing. I tried acupuncture, electro stim, heat and ice, a healing massage from a yoga guru, a Chinese recipe skin rub, a vinegar procedure to draw swelling away, manipulation of foot joints by multiple physical therapists, and good old-fashioned rest. Nothing worked.

It was well into the third month that the orthopedic surgeon recommended a cortisone injection to be administered directly into the nerves between my metatarsals. I was warned that this process should only be done once in any one spot, as it can cause breakdown of tissue. This made me desperate but hopeful. Dr. Hamilton administered the shot and told me to wait 24 hours, then to go ahead and put my pointe shoes on and try to give myself a slow barre workout. To my relief and surprise, the cortisone was a success. From that day forward my foot never felt nerve pain again.

Injuries are part of our existence and can be used as a learning process. We instinctively know how to set goals and how to execute them. It's the same process with an injury. You take it one day and one step at a time. I learned to slow down my body and retrain my technique. I learned to trust my body when it said it was hurting. I learned to dance smart by knowing when to push myself and when not to. I learned to appreciate a healthy body.

SPOTLIGHT LESSON

There will always be a time when you feel you must go back to the drawing board and start from scratch. Don't lose faith by believing this is lost time that is slowing you down. When things aren't going as planned, get off the fast-paced train of emotion and pursue the uninvited break intellectually.

1. **Start with the basics.** When you face an injury or setback, go back to retrain with the basic technique behind everything you do. Approach and embrace the slow pace and controlled movements and the new, stronger muscle memory.
2. **Don't take anything for granted.** Anything can change at a moment's notice. Casting can change, your body can go from healthy to injured, and your mind can go from confident to insecure. Use these moments to give yourself a reality check and appreciate where you are and how far you've come.

Notes:

COME PREPARED

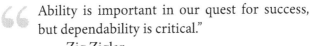

> Ability is important in our quest for success,
> but dependability is critical."
>   - Zig Ziglar

One afternoon, after I'd been dancing with the company for about four years, my rehearsals finished at 5:00 p.m., an hour earlier than usual. It gave me just enough time to walk the ten blocks to my apartment to rest for a while before returning to the theater for that night's performance. After weeks of physically-demanding, 12 to 13-hour days, my body and mind were conspiring for a chance to nap.

When I got home, I thought I'd just lay my head down for five minutes to rest. What seemed like seconds later, all of the peaceful bliss of slumber left me with a jolt. I awoke from my nap and my entire body went cold. My eyes felt like those of a cartoon character, jumping out of my head before springing back to their sockets.

My bedside clock read: 8:00 p.m. It was show time!

I'd missed our half hour call. I was scheduled to go on for the last ballet of the night at 10:00 p.m., but I wasn't in the theater warming up, putting on makeup, or preparing my costume. I was in bed! What was I thinking? I cursed under my breath as I power walked the ten blocks back to the theater. It was one of the few times I felt like other New Yorkers, who were always in a mad rush, and mad about *something*.

As I got closer to the theater, I started plotting: *I'll take the side elevator since that one isn't used as often. I'll go straight to the dressing room without stopping on stage to sign in, because* that *would just be giving myself away completely.*

I was sure my sweet friends had covered for me by writing my name on the sign-in sheet, and assured myself no one was looking for me. I used one of my reserve promise prayers—the kind you pull out for serious emergencies, like when you have the world's worst stomachache from eating too many cookies and you plead to God, "Please don't let me puke. Let me feel better. I promise I will never eat another cookie for the rest of my life." This called for one of those.

I approached backstage, begging God not to let me run into Peter or Rosemary. I arrived at the security desk, where the guards knew every dancer's face. "Deanna, it's 8:11," said the guard behind the desk.

I was jerked from my internal praying and swearing. "They've been calling your name over the intercom," he added, raising his brows. "They're looking for you. Better call up to stage and sign in."

So my friends *hadn't* signed me in! The guards buzzed me through the security door, and I waited impatiently for the elevator to come. Eventually it dinged, indicating the elevator was on street level, ready to pick me up. My body instinctively pulled a 007 move, flinging itself out of sight. I pressed my back flush against the wall and waited for the elevator doors to open. Once the coast was clear, my entire body sighed with relief as I slithered my way in.

I proceeded to press the button for the fourth floor dressing rooms, planning to bypass stage level where I might be spotted. All I needed was the elevator to go express to my dressing room, skipping all the other floors. If I could just get to the room's phone, I could call to stage level and fake that I'd been in the theater all along.

My luck ran out. The elevator stopped on stage level. I tried sinking into one corner, as if I could disappear into the wall, as Rosemary entered the elevator. My mission had been compromised! I was sure I was going to get reamed, but her expression took me by surprise—she was happy to see me! Her mouth opened and started to form words, but I was still in shock from her pleasant expression, and her words floated by without making any sense.

When I snapped out of it, she was busy organizing the next hour of my life. "I know you understudied *Mozartiana* when you were an apprentice three years ago. Do you remember it?"

This was a rhetorical question, of course. I was expected to remember it. "Four girls just finished the opening dance," she continued. "Dana sprained her ankle on stage. You'll have to fill in for her. We have only the pas de deux and male solo to get you ready and out there for the last section. Don't worry about makeup. There's no time. Get a pair of tights and pointe shoes and meet me in the wings A-S-A-P. Oh, and don't wait for the elevator, TAKE THE STAIRS!"

I was officially in a nightmare—one of those ballet anxiety dreams. Everyone was depending on me for the show to go on. Still in street clothes, I got off the elevator on the fourth floor and ran to the dressing rooms. The next several minutes went by at lightning speed.

I quickly pulled my hair into a slicked ponytail, not even bothering with a bun. I thought I would at least try to put my false eyelashes on, but my hands were shaking too much and the glue was oozing all over my lids. I gave up on that and gathered my pointe shoes and tights. I ran down four flights of stairs to the stage level.

Now was the ultimate test of multi-tasking. I stripped down in the wings on stage right, while someone from wardrobe helped secure a fake hairpiece into my hair, a baloney curl piece pinned tightly to my bun to make me look fancy. Its removal was quick, to help create an easy transition to the next ballet.

Heather Watts was side stage in the wings, and she frantically tied my feet into my pointe shoes. There wasn't a second to spare, because while all of this took place, Rosemary was spewing out an eruption of counts and steps to the ballet that I was to immediately and instinctively memorize.

"You *sauté* out from the wing and *pas de chat*. Wait 16 counts, then emboîté forward. You will blend past the other line of dancers coming towards you, and don't worry about the little girl on stage—she will look out for you."

She recited choreography for three minutes straight and I managed to absorb it all. As she continued relaying every detail, we ran down the narrow back passage to stage left, where I would wait and then enter in 24 counts. Rosemary knew the music so well, she could talk to me and count what was happening on stage at the same time. "Ok, this is your cue. Do you know what you're doing?"

"Um, sure," I muttered. I took the first jump on stage, my insides reverberating, and landed before 2,500 faces. After a few sequences of successful steps, with no mistakes or collisions, I paused on the side of the stage in a B+ pose. Head tilted in, arms held down to the side in a slightly curved shape. My weight on one leg, with the other crossed behind in a position of stillness and readiness all at once. I had four counts of eight to rest for the first time since I'd bolted out of my bed at home.

My mind drifted for a 10th of a second to my pale face without makeup. I wondered if anyone in the audience had noticed. Had they even noticed a dancer being injured? Soon enough though, my attention was drawn to the second wing, to Rosemary demonstrating my next 24 counts of choreography. This was a sight to see, as it had never happened before: Rosemary, clothed in an oversized *Cats on Broadway* t-shirt, dancing in the wings. There had been no time left for me to learn the rest of the movement before I'd gone on stage.

As I watched her, I unknowingly nodded my head in acknowledgment that I was absorbing what she was showing. I caught myself and stopped the jiggling. Then I was onto the next steps, making my way through the twirling figures around me. This on-the-spot training continued throughout the finale until the curtain came down with applause. I was drunk with disbelief. I hadn't missed a beat!

"Hey Deanna!" came a shout from over the applause. It was principal dancer Jock Soto, who had been watching the entire saga unfolding from the wings. He made his observation known to all: "Nice sheet marks on your face! Did we disturb you?"

It was sad but true. In the adrenaline rush of the evening, I'd failed to notice that my face was dented with creases from my nap. Leave it to a kind friend to point it out. Soon everyone was gathering around backstage to catch a glimpse of what live theater is all about: excitement.

It was a great feeling to have survived and conquered, to be depended upon and produce. It was the kind of adrenaline high that could last a week! You can draw upon moments like these later on, when things aren't going so well. These moments when you know you've surprised and surpassed yourself with your own abilities, when all of your previous discipline pays off.

SPOTLIGHT LESSON

Do you ever have moments where you lack confidence, or maybe your gut initially tells you a negative thought versus a positive pep talk? It can be hard to accept challenges if you put limits on yourself. Be someone who can be depended on.

1. **Practice being grateful.** Whenever you're given more than you think you can handle, try saying "I am grateful for this challenge." Gratitude turns any situation into a rewarding lesson. It brings a new perspective to a difficult situation.

2. **Make a list of your accomplishments to draw from.** It will help you in moments that seem to stretch your abilities. Keep a journal on the times you were proud of a certain accomplishment or outcome to remind yourself that you are someone who is available and dependable in moments of high expectation.

Notes:

NORMAL IS BORING

 I believe in serendipity, but I also believe there are times when you have to be the one who lines up everything so it can fall into place."
- Susan Stroman

Does one have to be crazy to be an artist? You know, a little off? I've taken notice that anyone who is truly a master at what they do is also...well, off-center. In the world of the arts, I've come across some eccentric people and wondered if there is a reason behind the metamorphosis of talented artist turned maniac. Not to say that there aren't those random people out there who were already nuts to begin with, but what does it take to go over the edge?

Maybe one starts out totally normal but becomes crazy because of the incessant self-critique, the never-ending pressure (because a true artist is never satisfied), and the meticulous tendencies that come from the demands of perfection. For dancers, it's agitated even further by the overabundance of adrenaline pumping six nights a week, 42 weeks a year, year after year.

The underlying question is this: Do I end up sacrificing myself, my sanity, and my soul for my art? The answer is yes. Normal is boring. The mere act of thinking you're going mad is a common and almost welcomed occurrence at New York City Ballet.

As ballet dancers, our job is to create illusions, to steer people into a fantasy world. The only way to do so is by opening up our outer shells and revealing our souls. Especially at New York City Ballet, the caliber of dancers and the demand on those dancers is so high that giving anything less wouldn't be enough. Unfortunately, giving more doesn't necessarily grant you a ticket out of the corps de ballet to principal status.

As a matter of fact, no one is there to protect your soul or to make sure you get it back after you've given it away on stage. Only you can do that, and it isn't easy. It requires a bundle of inner strength, frequent conversations with yourself (warning: may contribute to path down crazy road), and prayers to the one above. After all, a little spirituality never hurt. Once you have grounded yourself, refurbished your confidence, and feel ready to take on a higher challenge, then you can take the leap to demand what you want.

At strategically picked moments, I would talk with the director, Peter. It wasn't an easy task. Being 12 and alone in your dark basement with the boogie man would be less scary than a one-on-one conversation with a six-three, square-jawed, European dance legend who holds the fate of your career in his hands. The theater was my life and I'd dedicated myself so fully that I'd allowed the outside world to fade away. Because of this, every disappointment that happened within that building was magnified.

Casting lets me down. Is my life over?

I am the one they choose to continuously throw on
stage in an emergency replacement. Is the sky falling?

I've understudied a role for years and have never been
given the chance to perform it. Does the world
hate me?

I get pulled from a part. Should I go live in a cave?

This is why being a true artist ultimately requires all of
your mental, physical and emotional investment.

New York City Ballet has approximately 100 dancers to
satisfy. They prefer if you don't take their decisions to heart.
The audience on the other hand, likes it when you can really
capture and engross them. The only way to do that is to
really care about what you are doing. And when you really
care about something, you take it to heart.

"Peter, there's something on my mind. Do you have three
minutes?" I asked, forcing my voice to be steady. My heart
pounded into my eardrums like a Metallica concert. We were
in the hallway outside the main studio. I had decided to
approach him after rehearsal. This convinced my nerves it
was less official, in a "let's talk over coffee" kind of way.

"Aha!" he exclaimed, in his typical magic trick tone. "I
have a meeting planned now but speak with Debbie (his
secretary) and make an appointment to see me."

The words slid out with a look of concern that only lasted
as long as the sentence. I nodded. I'd been half-expecting that
answer. As soon as he turned away, my ears stopped the
Lollapalooza concert and I was off to my next rehearsal.

The big talk was scheduled for two days later which just
gave me more time to get anxious as I mulled over my
concerns. I already knew what I wanted to say, but my mind
insisted on reiterating it day after day. I wanted to know

what I could do differently to challenge myself more, land non-corps roles, and get ahead. I was eager to prove myself. I had hopes, goals, desires and ambition. That is what motivated me each day.

I'd been in the corps for five years at this point, and I didn't want my career to become stale. I had given it time, and now it was time for more. In the company, there was no sure way to measure your advancement. You were as good as your last show, and even then, there's no guarantee you'll be cast again in the same role, especially if it's a solo or lead. You can't count on feedback, and there are never evaluations.

My mom always taught me to speak up for myself but I was never the aggressive type. My old philosophy: if someone is in charge, they must have a plan and I need to wait it out. I had a plan B philosophy as well: if that someone in charge didn't have me included in their plan, then I would have to intercede with my own two cents before closing any doors.

The big day came for the meeting with Peter. I gathered my thoughts and took a deep breath before walking down the long narrow hallway from my dressing room to the offices on the fourth floor. The hallway was actually the fly floor above the stage, where the stagehands hung out and worked on the lights and scenery. The stagehands would always greet me with a friendly smile as I passed by. That particular day, their warm greetings were especially welcomed and helped to calm my nerves.

I wanted to know if the director I was working for viewed my future the same as I did and if not, then what could I do to change his mind? My main focus was to get some feedback and to have an opportunity to express myself. I had felt ready for a new and challenging role for a while, and it hadn't come on its own.

When I arrived at his door, it was cracked open slightly. I

didn't immediately go in, as I needed to lurk outside for a few moments to gather my gumption. After a handful of deep yoga breaths, I entered.

He was sitting at his desk, looking over papers with his owl-eye-rimmed reading glasses. Judging by the thickness of the lens, he couldn't see a thing without them. Sometimes whispers would go around before a performance as to whether or not Peter had his glasses on. If he didn't, we didn't have to stress about him seeing all of our mistakes.

"Aha!"

He stood up from his desk as he noticed me enter and motioned me to join him on his couch—an infamous bright red leather, L-shaped piece that remained a permanent fixture in his office for decades.

As I sat down, I imagined the conversations he'd had with other dancers on the same couch. I wondered whether he possessed a fortune teller's eight ball to see into our futures.

"So..." he said, pausing. "You wanted to speak with me."

It was a commanding statement rather than a question. His whole presence was commanding with his sharp Eastern European bone structure, his deep voice with a hint of a Danish accent, and his hands, so expansive they could palm my head like a basketball. He'd used them occasionally in rehearsals in order to place us where he wanted us to be.

"I was hoping to talk to you about what I'm feeling, and I'd like your opinion on my progress," I said, my heart racing.

His head nodded three times but no words came out. My collection of bobble head figurines came to mind. "I'm feeling ready for a challenge."

He hesitated. "Are you asking me for a part?"

I gave him a hopeful look. "No, but if that's how it works...okay, yeah!" Luckily, he laughed along with me.

"No, honestly, Peter. I want to know if you have anything

in mind for me that will be coming up in the repertoire. And, well, where do you see me going?"

He gave me one of his vague answers. "Aha. Well Deanna, you know there are a lot of 16-year-olds in this company..."

I was 23 and for the first time, I started to feel like an old fart. He continued with his theory. "I have been trying to challenge and test the new girls…"

New girls? I was only five years into the company! If I was an old girl, then where was my senior discount? Why would one invest in a race horse only to keep it behind the gate? I began to question where he was going with this.

"What I'm saying is…there's a lot of competition." Was he testing my determination?

"I'm not intimidated with competition, Peter. I'm competitive with myself. I can take on a challenge."

The ball was in my court and I felt like I needed to elaborate, convince, and go in for the kill. "I know you've been happy with my corps roles and continue to cast me in every ballet, every night. I believe I can prove to you that I can handle a solo."

"Ah, well, there are some parts I can hand you but they are so fitting to you that it would just be like patting you on the back. It wouldn't be a challenge."

Was this a game of twister with my head? My point was precisely that: I just wanted a part where I could stand out for my strengths and prove myself. Who cared if it wasn't a challenge?

"Peter, I would be fine with a 'pat on the back.' It's a start."

"Deanna, I know you are a hard worker, and I like you. I like your dancing. We can depend on you. But there are other dancers that I have to give these parts to first because if I didn't give them something to do, they would be sitting in McDonald's eating french fries all day."

Had he really just said that? Was I understanding it correctly—a yearning for soggy, greasy, yellow nubs in a box was all it took? One had to have a weakness in order to get rewarded with a solo part?

"There are a few dancers that I asked to lose weight and they have, so now I have to reward them."

Yup, confirmed. Quick then, what the heck is my vice? I'd always kept a handle on my weight, so that wouldn't pass. I racked my brain, actually hoping to come up with a terrible, weak habit.

My eyes shifted around the room while I self-analyzed, trying to grasp for a brilliant vice. I almost said, "Guess what —I'm an ex-con! That's right, an ex-con! Yes. Yes I am, and I need your help." How twisted is that? I was instigating my own lunacy.

My time was up. He chimed in. "You know what I think? I think you are too ambitious," he cautioned, faulting me.

That was it! That was my vice! I had a moment of relief— I had a vice and would therefore be rewarded. But wait a second. *Too* ambitious? He made it sound like a bad thing. Even worse, I almost believed him that it was.

The conversation was certainly devoid of anything normal, and once again I was getting closer to insanity as I struggled to block the doubts in my head that I wasn't getting anywhere.

"You have to prepare yourself for disappointments because you have such high hopes."

Here is where the tears started. I was just so emotionally invested in my dancing. Although there was something therapeutic in letting the tears out, I felt frustrated by my vulnerable reaction. I'd wanted to appear strong.

"Peter, my high hopes are what make me strive and work hard each day. I like to think I'm climbing a ladder and learning a little more each day, each performance. If I can't have hope, then I've just been zapped of my reason for being here. I'm not satisfied just doing corps roles. Some people are, but I'm not. I don't want to be stagnant. I don't need the title. I don't need to be promoted. I just want the opportunity and the experience, as well as the fulfillment of someone having faith in me. That someone being you."

It's not like he was impossible to talk to. He had, after all, made himself available for the meeting. But I had to fight for myself. I waited for him to flinch but he didn't. He was slowly digesting what I had spewed out. Then he moved. Without any words or resolution, he stood up and motioned me towards the door. He gave me a token, a one armed hug that was more like a shoulder squeeze from a distant aunt. He hugged me and sent me on my way.

That was it, conversation over. As I sat in the dressing room afterward, the conversation continued inside of my head. I stared at my face in the makeup mirror, trying to grasp what had just happened. I couldn't find any positive conclusion until after my mind had replayed the entire scene 20 times. By the end of that day, I came to a palpable conclusion: my hope would carry me through all my corps work until the time came for my chance.

At New York City Ballet, chances came in two forms: good chances, and chances that could lead to good. Good chances were when they cast you for a solo or lead role because they believed in you. Chances that could lead to good were being an understudy and getting solo parts on less than a day's notice when someone got injured. This usually meant no more than an hour of rehearsal, but with the same level of pressure to do well as if it'd been your part from the beginning. It was those scary chances that eventually came to me on multiple occasions.

Being cast by decision or by default didn't matter to me. I was willing to do it all. You can't be picky with opportunity.

It may come to you in a form you didn't envision or prepare for in advance, but sometimes the only way to succeed is to show up to the party!

SPOTLIGHT LESSON

Do you ever feel like it's a struggle to keep your hopes high without losing perspective? Dealing with rejection or being denied can either limit you or encourage you to truly know and define your strengths and your weaknesses.

1. **Develop your authenticity.** Inner strength keeps your sanity in check. Don't lose your identity to your artistry. Rather, you should enhance your identity with your artistry. It's hard to knock down someone who truly knows their identity and goals.
2. **Always persevere.** If you shoot for the stars, then no matter your circumstances, you will land somewhere other than where you are now. You may learn more about yourself through that experience, or you just may land on that star!

Notes:

NO EXCUSES

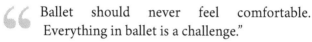 Ballet should never feel comfortable.
Everything in ballet is a challenge."
- George Balanchine

It was winter season. We had just finished five weeks of *The Nutcracker* and were smack in the middle of nine weeks of repertoire. In those nine weeks, we would perform three or four ballets a night for a total of 45 different ballets. Each evening's program was different so that our audience would always get a variety. In a typical winter season, I would be involved in 35 of the 45 ballets. It was a blessing and a curse to be a quick learner and hard worker: I was able to dance more than most of the other corps, but I was also the one they called on in an emergency.

I was expected to learn and perform a ballet in as little as 45 minutes. Over the years, I had learned to naturally absorb choreography at a fast-forward pace, simply because there was no other option. It's not like I could say, "No thanks, that won't be enough time for me."

After the three hours of emergency rehearsal is up, there

is no turning back. The performances are live, so you better have your brain on high alert and your eyes wide open. Not only are you under pressure to save the ballet from doom, but you are also judged by an audience that has no clue of the crash course chaos that just went on behind the curtain. And even more frustrating, the limited rehearsal time can leave little room for perfecting your artistry.

On one particular day, it all came around to bite me in the butt. It was a Saturday, a two-show day. It was a hard haul to carry after a long week of rehearsals and performances. Quickly, I had learned it was less draining to neither look ahead nor behind, but to just take it hour by hour, day by day. Each performance counted because each day was a new audience, excluding the *balletomanes* who made it a ritual to come every night. It was always the audience's applause and support that gave me that needed boost of energy.

The ballet *Donizetti* was scheduled to be on the program that day for the matinee and again in the evening. I was excited because I liked my part—there was a "three-girl" dance that would single me out similarly to a solo. I thought back to the past summer season when I was thrown into the same part in an emergency due to the injured dancer. I had a whopping three hours to learn the choreography as head girl of the corps. But this time, I'd been given enough time to prepare and perfect it.

Once I had applied my makeup and warmed up, I was ready for the afternoon performance. *Donizetti* was scheduled as the second ballet on the program. The music in *Donizetti* is sweet and energizing, and the choreography allows for a lot of personality, which makes it extra fun to dance. We got through the opening section of the ballet and all was fine.

When it was time for my "three-girl" dance, the music abruptly and unexpectedly sped up. I was trying to be playful and musical—which the choreography calls for—but I was also focusing on being precise and clear with my technique. I had to talk to myself as I danced, *stay with the music but don't let it rush you. Stay on top of it. Don't throw it away.*

My body and my thoughts were on hypersensitive alert. If a fly were to have zoomed at me, I swear I would have caught it between my fingers. I was on top of every beat of that music. We were sweating like three naked ladies in a sauna. When the curtain finally came down and intermission began, I stayed on stage for an extra two minutes to practice the steps that I wasn't allotted time to perfect. For me, I don't like leaving my body with a less-than-perfect feeling. I repeated the step until I was satisfied that my muscles memorized an exact and acceptable sensation.

As I turned to the wings to leave stage, Peter was standing there, still observing. "Your leg was too low in arabesque."

He had taken me by surprise, but I welcomed the correction and redid the step for him. "Yes, that's right, but you didn't do that before."

The obvious came pouring out of my mouth first. "The music was so fast, I would have been late for the next step if I'd done a higher leg."

He made a disappointed face and shrugged before exiting the stage. I realized he hadn't been looking for an excuse and quickly retorted to his back, "I'll be better tonight."

I got out of costume on stage level (where all the corps girls changed), and went back to my dressing room on the fourth floor. I decided not to let Peter's disappointment discourage me. After all, the next show was in less than three hours and I had to have my energy up—*Donizetti* would be first on the program.

I left my makeup on and walked to get myself a sandwich from the deli across the street. They were used to seeing dancers in full, caked-on makeup ordering takeout. I brought my food back up to my empty dressing room to eat and read about the latest fashion do's and don'ts in a magazine, when there was a knock at the door—it was Rosemary.

I gave a muffled, turkey-filled response. "Come in."

She entered and got straight to the point. "Deanna, I'm sorry, it's not my decision, it's Peter's. He asked that I replace you tonight in *Donizetti*. It would make life easier on me to not have an emergency rehearsal to replace you, but I have scheduled one for right now in the main hall."

I was shocked by his rash decision and lack of warning. I had never been pulled from a role. I couldn't help but become defensive. "I don't understand. Did he give you a reason?" I felt like I was reciting script from a TV drama.

"No, but he wants it this way," she said apologetically.

I wasn't convinced that he was convinced with his decision. "What if I spoke to him? Can I go to his office? It couldn't be something I can't improve by tonight."

Under normal circumstances, it's frowned upon to break silence and have a voice or opinion. This was a private circumstance, and as far as I was concerned, it would be a shame not to stand up for myself. I felt like my world was deflated, like I was being punished and sent to my room without dinner. My inner thoughts began coaching my confidence: *No matter what happens, maintain your confidence. You have other ballets that you have to dance in front of him for the rest of the season. Don't get emotional, he doesn't react well to tears. Don't take it personally, it's an isolated decision. Don't accept a rash decision, show him you're strong and up for the challenge.*

There were too many thoughts with too little time. It was just a straight walk from the dressing room down the long, gray concrete hall to his office. No posters, no flowers, no people—it was just me, the pit in my stomach, and the echo of my shoes. I spotted him standing in front of his office, looking like a stone statue as he watched me approach.

"Rosemary has informed me that I am being replaced," I said.

His body became tense and he automatically tried to shorten our conversation by answering with abruptness. "Yes, it was *my* decision."

"If you can tell me what it was that you didn't like, I can change it and it will be better tonight."

I was hoping he would soften his punishment. It was as if I was trying to talk my way out of a speeding ticket with an aggravated cop, only this was more personal. Slightly beet-faced and more determined, he objected to my challenging his decision.

"Your arabesque was too low! Horrible!"

"It was important to me to stay on the music," I said. "I know now that you prefer that I don't sacrifice the height of my leg. Can I please have the chance to apply your correction?"

We were still standing in the hallway, though he was slinking into his office and shutting the door slowly, obviously relaying the message that this conversation is going no further. He decided to make one last point. "I'm not going to put you in front of 2,500 people for you to practice."

I quickly computed that in my head to be 5,000 eyeballs. Now why would he think that I would want to disappoint 5,000 eyeballs? He continued on this alleged accusation. "That's what rehearsal is for."

It was going downhill as I continued to defend myself. "Peter, I prefer to challenge myself rather than walk away from something. I want your input and I want to improve. You've given me a correction, and now I'm asking for a chance to apply it. Knowing that 2,500 people are watching will only drive me more to do better."

"I make the decisions around here, not you!" he shouted.

The door slammed behind him. The sound echoed and I

turned into a mime with a painted black tear from mascara. As it rolled down my cheek, I thought to myself, *at least I can be happy about one thing, the tears stayed in until now.*

I guess this is all part of the career. Our next step and what path we take really does lay in the palm of the director. We are all at attention and we are all literally, only as good as our last performance.

SPOTLIGHT LESSON

Don't let one bad moment define you. We all have moments that are not up to par. We may strive for perfection in our craft and that is okay. We are especially vulnerable to judgement when we are part of a live art form. Just remind yourself that art is subjective and opinions can change daily based on the day's performance. We can choose to get caught up in one "off" moment, and give it more weight than it deserves, or we can choose to recognize the disappointing moments and allow growth.

1. **Never doubt yourself even when others doubt you.** Doubt destroys courage. Know what you are capable of and tell yourself you will be better next time.
2. **Get a fresh approach.** Start each new day as a day to do better. Pass any limits that were put upon you the day before.

Notes:

NEVER LET YOUR GUARD DOWN

 Great art has always been about saying a giant
'YES' to life."
- Rodney Smith

I'd finally gotten a new cell phone! I liked my number this time—it was easy to remember. Of course, now I had to update my information with every friend I had, and I'd inevitably end up on someone's blacklist for forgetting to add them. And God forbid the company couldn't get in touch with me for an emergency rehearsal or anything along those frantic lines.

"Don't do it, Deanna. Don't give the office your new number," Jason Fowler chimed in with his million-dollar advice.

"I know, right? I was thinking I would just let them implant a microchip into my neck instead. It'd make it easier to track me that way."

"Don't think they haven't thought of that. Their goal is to interrupt you in the middle of dinner to get you into a swan costume—you know that. You remember what happened last week to Miranda? She was on her second glass of wine when she got summoned in to do lead swan! They don't let you say no."

"This is true. And she still had a stellar performance!"

Here's the truth—there's no rest for the weary. Dance is a live art form and as dancers, we were on call every day and night, just like doctors. It was rare that a corps dancer wouldn't be cast in every ballet, and therefore had a night off from performing. So obviously, when that rare night did come along, one had to take full advantage. However, the "reach out and touch someone" obligation overwhelmed me and I caved. I gave my new number to the office— pronouncing one slow number at a time, in a desperate cling to the private digits.

"They will appreciate your honesty and professionalism one day Deanna, and you will be rewarded," Fowler uttered facetiously.

"Thank you, Fowler, for my recommended daily allowance of sarcastic support."

As luck would have it, that coming weekend was Super Bowl Sunday and I wasn't cast to dance. I could cash in my chips and enjoy a day off, provided I didn't have any rehearsals. The performance was at 3 p.m. on Sunday and rehearsals ran from 11 to 1:30 p.m. Typically, if they wanted to rehearse any ballet that would be performed the following week, they would rehearse it on the Sunday before the show. Since our rehearsal schedule was never posted until 8 p.m. Saturday evening, there was no way to make advanced plans for a day off.

Still, I was desperate to make plans for the Super Bowl. I wanted to be with my boyfriend at the time, who lived two hours away in Philly, PA. He had a party planned at his apartment and wanted us to spend the day together. So there I was at Saturday evening's show, checking the schedule board backstage at every exit and intermission, in hopes of catching Sunday's schedule. The schedule finally went up when the performance ended at 11 p.m.

I quickly scanned it, checked it, double-checked it, and double-scanned it—I was off! Not only was I excused from Sunday rehearsals, but I also didn't have to understudy any of the ballets that were in Sunday's program. That meant I didn't even need to be around my phone, or "on-call," so to speak.

The next day, I caught an early morning train to Philly. At 8 a.m. I found myself full of energy as I boarded the Northeast Corridor line to Trenton, PA, and eventually onto Philly. This was a route I had gotten very familiar with since dating my boyfriend. For the amount of money I used to spend on NJ Transit, I should've bought stock in it as soon as we started the long-distance relationship.

The train arrived in Philly at 11:30 am. He picked me up at the station and drove me back to his apartment. After two cups of coffee and three hours on the train, my bladder was going to burst. The second we walked through his door, I ran to the bathroom. The moment I sat down on the toilet, my cell phone rang in the living room.

From the other side of the bathroom door, my boyfriend yelled, "It's a 212 area code!"

"NYC!" I shouted. Blood shot up my veins with each trailing ring. All of my friends would be busy dancing in class at that time of day, leaving only one possibility—it was the theater.

They never called unless they needed a replacement, and I dreaded the idea as I let the phone ring again. I hurried into the living room and stood over my phone, engaging in a game of charades with my boyfriend. Screeching facial expressions at phone meant: *I don't want to answer it!*

Wrinkled brow and eyes darting from him to the phone and back to him meant: *Help me!*

With another ring, it was time to decide. I could either let them leave a voicemail and then see how urgent it really was, or I pick up and respond unprepared. I took too long to decide and they were kicked to voicemail. I made one last undying claim to my boyfriend, "It's the company! And there's something you need to know—I traded my soul."

"I thought you said there wasn't a chance you'd be needed today?"

"You're right, you're right, you're right."

The first "you're right" was to console him, the second was to convince myself, and the third was just a statement of rebellion and conviction that was short-lived. The phone beeped to indicate a message, and I dialed my voicemail. My boyfriend and I put our cheeks together so we could both listen.

"You have one new message. You have two saved messages. New message is from outside caller."

The automation clicked to Rosemary's voice. "Where are you? It's Rosemary. *Square Dance* can't go this afternoon. We need to change the program. Peter wants to put *Serenade* on and it's going first in the program. We need you. Call me as soon as you get this. It's 11:45."

Great. Just when I thought I had successfully and slyly skipped town, I was caught. My boyfriend tried to be helpful, but he didn't understand that the company didn't take "no" for an answer.

"It's almost impossible to get you back in time—the show starts in three hours. It would take you three hours by train and that's if you leave this moment. Just tell them you're in Philly and can't make it."

"I have to call them now! The sooner I call, the more time it gives us all to figure this out. I'm sorry. This sucks."

I called Rosemary back and got her assistant, Tommy. "Hi, it's Deanna. Is—"

"Deanna! We tried to reach you," he interrupted. "Where are you?"

"Philadelphia?"

"And *why* are we in Philadelphia?"

Did he really want the full story of how I was struggling to have a social life? "I know. So it's bad timing. Can I speak with Rosemary?"

Rosemary took the phone with her constructive voice of reason and, as always, direction. "Deanna, I hear you are in Philadelphia. Can you get someone to drive you here in time for three o'clock curtain? Call me back to let me know. I won't tell Peter unless I have to. If you don't think you can, I will have to tell him so that we can switch *Serenade* to be last on the program, but obviously that's not ideal. Let's aim for you to make it here and be ready for three o'clock. Call me if things change."

If we were playing Scrabble, she would've easily won with the amount of words she'd managed to fit in. I, on the other hand, had fit in only one deep inhale. Zero points.

I only had one option—Bob. My boyfriend's roommate Bob had a car, and it just so happened that he was still sleeping off a crazy night out with friends.

"We need to wake up Bob," I said. "Do you think he'd let us drive his car? I would need to leave now in order to arrive in time to do makeup and warm up."

Thank God for Bob. He actually volunteered to drive me himself. Since his girlfriend lived outside of the city, he used it as an excuse to surprise her. I was calm this whole time until Bob—apparently unaware of the emergency of the situation—decided to grab a long, hot shower first. But it wasn't Bob's fault. It's hard for others to comprehend a dancer's life sometimes.

We didn't peel out of the apartment's parking lot until 12:45 p.m.— just two hours and 15 minutes until curtain. I made the requested phone call to Rosemary to let her know we were on the road. Bob miraculously got us from Philadelphia to Manhattan in under an hour and a half—and by 'miraculously,' I mean we didn't see a single cop as we broke the speed record on the NJ Turnpike.

Once we got to the theater, I thanked Bob and went our separate ways. I flashed my ID as I ran past security. I would've missed the elevator if my ninja hand hadn't slid between the closing doors.

The doors opened back up to reveal Peter. Of course. Despite my traffic updates and Rosemary's earlier promise, she had apparently filled Peter in on my secret agenda. "Aha. You made it." He unraveled the fact like he had just solved the day-old mystery. "What if you couldn't be contacted and didn't get here?"

This came out more as a warning than a true question, so I avoided giving him a true answer. I went with a witty comeback to repeat his detective-like enthusiasm.

"Aha, but I am here. That's what counts, right?"

It worked. He responded acceptingly, "Yes. That's right! You are right!"

Now came the challenge of being ready for the show. This meant being in stage makeup, hair slicked-back into a tight bun, toes taped to prevent blisters, body warmed-up, in-costume with pointe shoes on and ribbons sewn closed, as well as a quick review of the steps. In 45 minutes.

This process typically took me twice that time. My friends all offered to help me in any way they could to speed things up, because we all lived by the philosophy that anything can be done. That's the way it worked around there. And despite any series of unfortunate events, we would make it happen.

"There's a hole in the bucket, dear Liza, dear Liza!" Carrie Lee jokingly sang out, waiting for my response.

I knew the children's song well and sung back the next verse enthusiastically, "Well fix it, dear Henry, dear Henry!"

So we did—we fixed it. There was a last-minute hole in the program and we fixed it without a hitch. It was actually one of the best *Serenade* performances I had ever done. A lot can be said for dancing under extra adrenaline and less prep time. Sometimes too much time gives room for nerves, anticipation, overanalyzing, and over-practicing. This particular performance left no room for excess, only pure dance. For that brief 40 minutes on stage, I forgot about what the rest of the world was thinking about— football.

SPOTLIGHT LESSON

Ever feel like you've let your guard down and maybe made a poor choice along the way? If you get distracted from your focus there is always a way to redeem. Look for it.

1. **Never give up.** There is no rest for the weary. The show must go on, so learn to be ready at all times in posture, expression, and energy level to reveal your commitment.
2. **Always land on your feet.** Every employer wants an employee who thinks outside the box when there is a hitch in the road. Learn to think of solutions for every obstacle.

Notes:

GEOFFREY BEENE

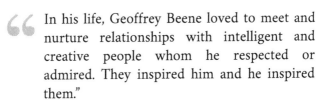

> In his life, Geoffrey Beene loved to meet and nurture relationships with intelligent and creative people whom he respected or admired. They inspired him and he inspired them."
>
> - Kim Hastreiter in the book *Geoffrey Beene: An American Fashion Rebel*

Exposing yourself to other forms of art can enhance an already focused artistry. I always felt it was important to broaden myself, as opposed to having tunnel vision. In the arts, everything has a common ground. It all links together as inspiration and one long learning experience of self-discovery. So to me, delving into acting classes, singing lessons, and most dear to me, the fashion world, opened my eyes and made my dancing more dynamic.

It all started with one designer: Geoffrey Beene, fashion's classic of which there is no clone. Beene was looking for a way to present his latest collection: soft jersey evening gowns that flowed with every move, practical one-piece evening jumpsuits, and some of the most original, painting-like boleros and cloaks. His masterpieces were gorgeous, comfortable, flexible, and one of a kind.

His vision was to photograph dancers leaping, lunging, and doing what they do best while wearing his clothing, to accentuate the flexibility of the evening wear.

At the time, in the spring of 1992, I was still an aspiring ballet student. Geoffrey Beene and his assistants had chosen to visit the School of American Ballet in order to pick a lucky handful to be models for a day. The timing couldn't have been worse—my family taking an obligatory trip to California to visit relatives. I had to put the idea of being a model out of my head and leave town with my family. Only in New York City could there ever be enough to do to make one *not* want to go on vacation.

I tried to enjoy myself in California, but I couldn't help but think of what I was missing, and how much I would've loved to be part of the fashion world. When I was back in ballet classes a week later, I stopped by the office, thinking there might be a slight chance Geoffrey Beene hadn't picked dancers yet. I volunteered to make a trip to his studio to meet him, if the office would call ahead and stall the decision process.

I figured that worst case scenario, I would at least be able to meet him. And in the best case, I would be chosen. Typically, I'm not that bold, but when fate plays a hand, it acts like a magic web that compels one to do what they do.

I arrived at the building address the office had given me and stared up to the 2nd floor where Beene's studio was. It was one big wall of glass, with *Beene* scrolled across the window. Through it, I could see a model standing with her back to the street. *They must be in the middle of a photo shoot,* I thought to myself. *How exciting.*

I tried imagining myself in that spot, the sun beams

reflecting off of what looked like a silver-painted wall beside her. I walked up the stairs to the 2nd floor, where I came to a glass door. I walked in and stood at a receptionist's desk, where a red-headed assistant sat glued to the phone.

"Hi dear," she called out, but I missed my 1/8th of a second window to respond as she continued her phone mania.

"Geoffrey Beene, please hold."

"I'm back sweetie. Yes dear, his driver, at 3:30, yes. One second."

"Good morning, Geoffrey Beene. Well get rid of them. They are tacky and overpriced anyway."

She continued to talk while throwing her hands into the air in a gesture of hopelessness. I turned my glance to the room and the artsy sketches on its walls. They were hand-painted portraits of elongated, suave models in striking poses, created by the well-known artist Joe Eula. I loved being surrounded by such creativity.

The red head with the New York accent redirected her conversation back to me. "Look at your flawless skin. You don't wear any makeup do you sweetie?"

Oh, but I did. I had been wearing foundation and blush all over my face since I was 10 because my teachers would send me home from school and tell my mom, "She's so pale, she must be sick." No, just Irish.

"Your skin is like a baby," she continued. "Not me. I couldn't get away with wearing no makeup—or I should say, I would scare my husband without it. And this, honey," she said, grabbing a tuft of her hair, "is a wig. Oh, you didn't know that."

Once again, I was given no chance to respond as she put the phone back to her ear. "Joyce, Geoffrey Beene. Yes, just bring them here and George will do something with it. Oh sweetie, please, you know me…"

I was in no rush. I was fascinated by the way she made being on the phone an actual art form. She had full control of her high-tech, 12-line mechanism that seemed to have a personality of its own. She was precise and business-like with everyone on the other line, but she didn't leave her personality behind.

Finally, the calls stopped. "Oh it comes in waves, sweetie. It goes on like this all day. And Mr. Beene knows I'm the only one who can handle this." I didn't doubt her. "You should see the chaos when I'm sick. But he knows—that's why I have to come in with my box of Kleenex and Lysol spray if that's the case. He wouldn't let me stay at home. So how can I help your pretty face?"

"I'm a ballet dancer from the school where Mr. Beene observed some classes last week. I was hoping that I might still have a chance to be seen."

"Alber will help you. How old are you? You look 12." She buzzed Alber Elbaz through the door.

"I'm 17," I answered. "I know I don't look my age."

"You're a baby, just a baby. You'll be happy when you're... oh Alber, honey."

Alber strutted into the room with raised eyebrows. Joyce's head snapped back to me. "What's your name, honey?" she asked.

"Deanna." As I said it, I caught myself wondering whether my name sounded artsy enough. Maybe I should have told her it was Anastasia or Penelope?

She turned back to Alber. "Deanna is here to have her picture taken for that ballet thing. Did Mr. Beene give you the Polaroid? Can we just take one of Deanna to add to the pile?"

A few minutes later, I was smiling for a Polaroid camera. My modeling future was in the hands of a Polaroid picture. Just one picture—no "do-overs."

After the picture, Alber thanked me and off I went. I turned to say goodbye to Joyce, but she was back on the phone. She waved goodbye with her salon-enhanced nails, leaving behind a mirage of a rainbow in the air.

That was the beginning of my modeling adventure. They chose me and three other girls from my class to be photographed for a June exhibit.

———

The photo shoot was a 13-hour day that started with makeup at 8 a.m. Sam, the makeup artist, had two hours to finish all four of us.

"Luckily, Mr. Beene likes simplicity. Girl, I don't know what they're thinking sometimes when they put time limits on makeup! It'll be done when it looks good. All of you make my job easy with your easy breezy CoverGirl skin. You're like dolls. Is that because you sweat a lot? I should take you all home and put you on display in my china cabinet. Speaking of dolls, I collect Barbie dolls, so if any of you have any to sell..."

He continued chatting with us as he primped us with makeup. Soon we would learn that anyone working for Mr. Beene would abide by his visions, not their own. Mr. Beene was there to give his input on every aspect of the shoot. He stood in the background with a quiet demeanor, speaking up only when he felt it necessary to lead.

This happened once or twice with the makeup artist: "No, I don't want too dark of lips and bleach out the eyebrows all together. No distractions from the pure features."

It also happened with the photographer: "No, don't take pictures that you think you would like to have in your portfolio, only what I ask you to take. I want this dress moving, not stagnant."

As far as the dancers were concerned, we were given creative liberty. Beene was mesmerized by the fusion of ballet and fashion, as was I. He told the photographer, "They are birds that need to fly. Let them do their thing and you just be ready to capture it."

Once our eyebrows were cut, tweezed, shaped, and bleached, with our lipstick the "perfect" shade, we were photographed one at a time. When it came to my turn, one of the male assistants needed to pin my skirt from the inside so that it would hang just right. He knelt down, reached his hands up my skirt, and began pinning away at my butt. I must have given an awkward look to the photographer, Andrew Eccles, because he just smiled at me and started singing, "Getting to know you, getting to know all about you…"

We all cracked up. It's funny what becomes acceptable depending on the industry you're in.

A few hours into the shoot, and without a change of makeup, Sam grew bored. "We need a TV in here. And by TV I don't mean television, I mean transvestite!"

He bounced to a beat in his head as he powdered our faces and refreshed our makeup one last time before he was given authority to leave. Mr. Beene didn't stay until the end of the shoot either. He left a little after lunch, only once he trusted that he had all the shots he was looking for and that we were in a good flow.

By 9 p.m. we had taken over 700 pictures. I was wired and inspired. I didn't want it to end. It was like magic—the way so many art forms could come together in one picture.

The exhibit took place in June, in one of our ballet studios in the Rose Building at Lincoln Center. The chosen photographs were blown up and displayed around the room. The couture items featured in each photograph were displayed next to the photo, on wire bodices.

The event was invitation only and open to the press. The four of us were dressed in jumpers especially designed for us by Mr. Beene. We were positioned in the studio amongst the displays to mingle, dance, and model for the intrigued visitors. My best friend, Michelle, came to show her support. She had been wandering around the exhibit, before coming back into my line of sight, rushing toward me.

"Deanna, there is a picture of you from the back that practically shows your boob! Don't worry. I spoke with one of the assistants. I told him I didn't think you would approve. He's looking into it."

"Michie, it's okay," I said, "Thanks, but it's okay. It's art. Not that I want to show off my boob cause there's really not much there, but it's just a profile outline. I saw it. The photo is more about the back of the dress and the scoop of the fabric."

I guess my experience modeling had trained my eye to see shapes of the body and the shapes of the fabric, where Michelle was just looking out for me. She knew of my shy side, which had now taken a fashion adjustment.

Alber came over to us just then and took me aside. I assumed he was going to speak to me about Michelle's concern. "Deanna, Mr. Beene would like to offer you a contract to continue modeling for him. He likes your work and hopes to continue the relationship."

Was I dreaming? Just two weeks prior I'd been just a student. And just in the previous week, I'd been offered an apprenticeship with New York City Ballet, my childhood goal. Now I was being offered a modeling contract! My honesty and naiveté spoke first.

"Alber, it's an honor. I would love to continue to work for Mr. Beene, but I just signed a contract with New York City Ballet."

As the words shot out of my mouth, I regretted them. I

couldn't lose this opportunity, but as a dancer you have very little time to spare for anything else. That was my practical brain taking over. I quickly brought that to a halt and summoned my determination to the stand.

"With my new company schedule I will only have Mondays off. If we can work together on Mondays, then that's a yes!"

"Mr. Beene will work around your schedule. He respects that," Alber replied.

I was thrilled to not have to say goodbye to modeling. I never regretted my decision—it was an amazing experience. I didn't let my focus narrow, and I didn't let one art get in the way of the other. I blended the two, enjoying how one breathed life into the other. Mr. Beene and I worked together regularly from that day on, for more than a decade. Eventually, I became the girl in the window on 57th street, with the sun beaming in on me as I danced in front of the silver walls for the beloved Mr. Beene.

Print ad for Geoffrey Beene. Photography credit Andrew Eccles.

SPOTLIGHT LESSON

You can find inspiration all around you, if you stay open-minded and learn to take in your surroundings.

1. **Broaden yourself.** Immerse yourself in inspiration from multiple angles. Whatever interests you— whether it be artwork, fashion, photography, books—take that inspiration and apply it towards enhancing your focused craft.
2. **Learn from other professionals.** Ask questions. Observe. Volunteer or intern. Share your art form and inspire others in order to grow further in your own craft.

Notes:

BALLET DANCER OR MOVIE STAR

Give me something to dance about and I'll dance it."
    - Jerome Robbins

I was three years into company life and doing my fair share of fun corps roles. I was even getting cast in some "senior corps roles," such as *Serenade* and *Concerto Barocco*. Life was fully challenging enough at the ripe age of 21; there was no need to add anything additional—unless of course it was going to be really, really exciting...like filming a movie!

"It's a television movie that involves a dancer!" Gina screeched. "The audition is next week over on 5th avenue somewhere. It's based on a Danielle Steele novel, Deanna! Four days of filming is all that's needed and that's all I know, except for the fact that you will get it if you audition. I just feel it in my bones!"

Gina, a very close friend, was always up on the acting scoop. She was living her dream, jumping from job to job in the acting industry. She was forever engrossed in the *Village Voice* and other audition notice outlets. She was a dancer herself, so she always passed along the "dancer" auditions to me as well. I had always shrugged them off, feeling plenty occupied by my workload at the company, but this time felt different.

Three years into the company, I believed management knew my work ethic well enough to realize that I was happiest when I was busy, that I didn't like to "let the grass grow between my toes." Besides, a little acting experience could help me further develop my personality on stage for dance.

"You know Gina, I just might consider this one." I nonchalantly threw out the words, but my eyes were widening at the possibilities. What if I was chosen for a mini series! What if this lead to more movie proposals!

"Listen," Gina chimed, juggling her bags and keys. "Call my coach, she will give you a session, and you'll be on your way."

She was off to an audition for a furniture commercial where she would have to act sexy with an arm chair. That would be a little too advanced of acting for me. She closed the door behind her, but she couldn't refrain from opening it one more time to ensure her artist's words of wisdom were heard. "If not for yourself Dee, then for the audience!"

As timing would have it, the audition was on a Monday, my one day off. I took it as a sign and went to the audition. Trying to remember all the cues and advice from Gina's coach, I felt official as I blabbed my lines under my breath while sitting on the subway, which also explained why all the seats around me were empty. I decided to shut my mouth and save it for the audition, but soon my flittering eyes and multiple facial expressions were silently speaking my lines for me again, not unnoticeably.

A skip up the subway stairs and three blocks later, I arrived at the audition site at 1515 Broadway, an apartment building with a large lobby. I headed to the 44th floor with a ballet headshot in hand and a makeshift resume in the other.

The small studio apartment was empty except for one table. Apparently they'd rented it out just for one day to conduct auditions. The scene reader was behind the table and the camera was angled at the seat that would soon be mine. The casting director greeted me with dissecting eyes, already analyzing whether I fit the role. After quick introductions, I read my lines for the camera. "I'm a dancer, a good dancer. It's what I've always wanted to do."

———

Tuesday morning started with a ballet class at 10:30 a.m. When class ended at noon, I received a notice from the office that a "Robin from casting" was trying to get in touch with me. I wondered whether management was onto me now, aware that I'd auditioned for something unrelated to them. Before I let myself get too concerned, I felt I should first find out what Robin wanted to say. I quickly called from the payphone next to the studio. Each ring without an answer added to my anxiety, until I heard a click.

"Hi, this is Deanna McBrearty. I received a message from your office to contact Robin regarding casting."

"Yes, Deanna," a woman's voice said. "You have been chosen for the role of a Russian ballerina in our Danielle Steele mini series. Filming will take place in four months in St. Petersburg, Russia. We will need you for four days of filming."

"Not Florida but Russia? St. Petersburg, Russia?" I asked, thinking I surely must've heard her wrong, as if Russia sounds so much like Florida.

"Yes. St. Petersburg, Russia."

I had no other questions. I was ecstatic! I thanked her and

said I would be in touch. I hung up and took off in a sprint to my *Harlequinade* rehearsal. I had tons of energy in my dancing that day, bubbly from the excitement, and put off the decision-making process until that evening.

I knew it would entail more than just a slick step into a successful career move; I would have to convince Peter that we would all benefit from the experience. I was up all night trying to figure out how to approach him, and how to get his permission to take four days off from spring season rehearsals. I knew I would be able to justify that at least it wasn't performance season. I wouldn't be missing any shows. I weighed my options over the phone with my mom.

"Put it in Peter's hands," she said. "Let him make the decision. See what his reasons are and go from there."

I needed back up. I called a long-time friend and past ballet teacher for her opinion. "I think it's a great opportunity that you shouldn't pass up."

All I could hope was that Peter would be as supportive, and maybe even a little accommodating. I slept on it and made an appointment with Peter's secretary the next morning.

Peter had me come to his office, where once again a decision would be made on the red leather couch. As he shut the door behind us, I felt the confidence of my speech seep out of me. He had a way of causing that.

"So, you wanted to see me." The words exhaled into one big sigh. I attributed this to his foresight that something must be up if he is sitting on his couch with one of his dancers.

"Yes," I said, not wanting to add details or create any suspense for purity's sake. I went right to my point. "I've been asked to play the role of a ballerina in a TV movie. They start filming this spring and it would require that I take four days off."

I would have continued with my out-of-breath convincing act, but he cut me off. "Ah. Mhm. Do you know what Balanchine would have said to me? He would have said, 'Dear, do you want to be a ballet dancer or a movie star?' We all have choices, so I ask you the same: Do you want to be a ballet dancer or a movie star?"

I replied without hesitation, "Both!"

He retorted, "So you want your cake and you want to eat it too."

"Sure, why not?" I asked, unflinchingly with a smile.

He fought back. "Well you see, if I allow you, I will have to allow others the same treatment. Then I will be left without anyone here."

"But no one else has been offered this opportunity but me," I said. "It's only four days and it will help my dancing, my confidence, and my name. It will bring press to the company!" I spoke with such urgency I forgot to breathe.

"I can't really say anymore you see, the decision isn't just up to me and you. You will need to speak with Rosemary."

My guess was Rosemary wouldn't look highly upon my outside interests. I was stuck in a hard place because I hated to make waves when things were going well for me in the company. I always wanted them to think of me as a hard worker and dedicated, but I also liked sticking out of the crowd and being different. I didn't want to blend in, and so maybe this was my shot to stand aside from the rest. I knew this wasn't going to be an easy conversation.

I walked down the hall from Peter's office and knocked on Rosemary's door. She tightly called, "Come in."

I entered to see her swing her chair sideways, away from her desk, to eyeball who it was. Once she realized it was a dancer, who had uninvitingly sprung upon her, she straightened her posture. "What is it?" she asked.

I expressed the same story to her as I had to Peter, only

timelier and with a little less detail, since she is more of the "Lipton instant soup that only takes a minute" kind, rather than the "ham and bean all day event" type. Her answer to me came spewing out only moments after the wires behind her eyes computed the consequences.

"We can't let you just take four days, you would have to take leave for the whole season. When you return you can't have your old parts back—you will have to go back to the drawing board. You are a quick learner, but it wouldn't be fair to the other dancers. If you have other interests, we can't make room for that."

I hadn't expected her to put up a wall, but where there's a will, there's a way—or at least that's how I approached my next utterance.

"Don't get me wrong. New York City Ballet has always been my dream. I'm not turning my back now. I don't want to make waves and I'm not asking for special treatment. It's just an opportunity that fell in my lap."

"So then" she added, "it would be gravy for you. You already have what you want, and this would just be gravy."

She was making it out to be messy gravy that was a sinful decadence. I saw it as rich gravy that would top it all off just right. But how do I continue trying to convince, when I may be hindering any future impression of myself?

"New York City Ballet was always my goal. Every day I work really hard, and I appreciate every role I've earned. I don't want to lose my place, I was just hoping—"

She abruptly hurried into my sentence. "There is your answer. Don't expect everything. We don't offer guarantees here."

She had ultimately left the decision up to me, but it came with a warning, like a blurb on a bottle of household cleaning supplies: If taken, there will be trouble.

Without a "thumbs up," I made the decision to turn down

the movie. Naturally, I did what I always do in order to feel better whenever something doesn't work out as I might have hoped—I created a moral to the story. Otherwise, I would have felt all was lost. The lesson learned this time around: not everyone is interested in your best interests. Once I realized this, I realized my future would be up to me, and only me. Obviously, it hadn't been the time for me to have "icing on my cake," but perhaps someday it would be my time to stand out.

Journal:
We need to feed our minds with conviction. Otherwise, we are only pretenders deceiving truth. If we try and take shortcuts through life's obstacles, we are—a majority of the time—making our lives more complicated.
Life happens and goes on no matter what, so we need to invite it in our way, before it pushes itself in another way.

SPOTLIGHT LESSON

You are responsible for the path your future takes, so put yourself in the driver's seat.

There will be times you may not agree with the opinions of others, or the direction they give you. Know that the final decisions are always yours, which is why it's important to take the time to truly know yourself, so you can best judge the outcome or resolution.

1. **Know your own truths.** Stand up for what you believe your goals are and for what matters to you most. There may be a variety of things you want to accomplish so do a cross check to maintain focus and cohesiveness in your goals.

2. **Know how to make a decision.** Weigh the pros and cons and be truthful to your strengths and weaknesses. Base your final decision off of that evaluation.

Notes:

JUGGLE OR STEP ASIDE

 Insanity: Doing the same thing over and over again and expecting different results."
- Albert Einstein

Every once in a while, a choreographer would come to New York City Ballet, ready to wrap his ideas around a chosen cast of dancers. This kept the company from becoming a museum of work. Instead, we presented the old favorites with the fresh and new. Being able to perform the same ballets over many years gave me a way to measure my progression: I felt a sense of accomplishment as I became more experienced with every year I performed them.

However, it was extremely refreshing to be part of a work in progress, where every step was created in the studio, in preparation for a world premiere. This excited me because I could make that part dynamically my own, instead of the pressure of living up to a past cast and their "memorable" interpretation.

It was that time of year when a choreographer would come around, and rumors were out that Eliot Feld would be coming back to create a new piece. I had previously worked with him on a revival of one of his older ballets, entitled *The Unanswered Question.* I'd had a great time working with him on that ballet, where I'd gotten to play the main part of "bicycle girl." I had worked many hours with him—first for the audition process and then while perfecting the part, which required much coordination. The choreography was all an illusion of soft arms and upper body, but it beat the pulp out of your thighs!

The prop was a six-foot high tricycle that I had to peddle and steer across the stage in seamless patterns, without holding onto the handlebars. Instead of the arms doing all of the steering, they were used for soft, flowing, circling por de bras. It was nothing like being a little tike on a bike. This seemed hard enough alone, but then Eliot added the weight of a muscular, male principal dancer sitting on the handlebars! Needless to say, it only took one rehearsal for every girl he chose to audition to blow out their quads and swear against the role. The pain set in for the following rehearsal day, convincing not a single dancer to volunteer to try it again.

Despite having to take six Advil that morning just to lower myself onto the toilet and walk down the stairs, I made myself the exception. I don't know why I volunteered, except not to look weak in Eliot's eyes—or maybe I'd been feeling slightly masochistic that day. I claimed I wasn't sore and got the part. Ultimately, I worked out all the kinks in rehearsals with either Damian Woetzel or Albert Evans on my handlebars, and of course Eliot always observing from the front of the studio.

Eliot nicknamed me "Durbin," as in the singer/actress Deanna Durbin. I took it as a sign of affection, and the nickname quickly spread so that some of the other dancers called me it as well.

Albert had apparently done this part 10 years ago when the ballet first went. "Hey Durbin, admire these..." Albert excitedly squeaked while pointing downwards.

I half expected to see a new Prada bag or Burberry leg warmers because Albert, with his oil-moistened muscles, only owned things that made him look good. He claimed he had a Prada bag that he kept in his porcelain bathtub at night in case there was ever a fire. But when I looked down at his feet, there wasn't anything Prada. "What! Crusty, blue, spray-painted ballet slippers? Where did you dig those up from?"

"That's right Deaaaaaanna!" he sang, dragging out the A in my name and giving it an English accent. "I did this ballet 10 years ago and I still had these shoes in my locker! Girl, they are welding my toes together but I have to wear them for opening night!"

I remember those times fondly: I adored working with Eliot, Damian, and Albert. And as we stood in the studio to meet our newest choreographer, I hoped to see Eliot stroll into the studio.

I smiled as a familiar head snaked around the doorway frame into the main hall studio where we were all in the middle of company class, our one-hour warmup used to prepare our muscles for the six-hour rehearsal day ahead. The snaking head belonged to Eliot Feld, and with scrutinizing eyeballs attached. So began the observation process of narrowing down his cast for his new ballet.

The next few days were auditions and rehearsals with Eliot and his dancer assistants instructing us in "Eliot-esque" movements. This went on for a week and he wasn't very patient with us. He wasn't the same friendly Eliot I had worked with before. I told myself that maybe he was better one-on-one than with big groups.

After one week of examining our talents, he chose his cast and a few apprentice stragglers to understudy. With 10 years of experience in the company and having worked with Eliot before, I'd thought I would escape the whole cattle call process otherwise known as auditioning. That, however, was a lesson to be learned in the corps. There were no guarantees and no special treatments. Eliot chose his cast of 24 corps girls, myself included, and began the staging of his ballet *Organon*.

On day one of rehearsals, I found myself confused with his movements. They were different and quirky, like broken doll spasms. They looked good on his assistants, but would take some time on our upright habits.

"C'mon girls. Stop being such sissy ballerinas! Embrace a new movement. You have to forego some things in order to achieve others," he croaked in his philanthropic way.

I realized then how necessary it was as a choreographer to have patience, because otherwise you create a very tense and unproductive atmosphere. It must be hard though when you envision one thing and keep witnessing another. However, it was still the early stages and it would all come with time, especially because he was dealing with professionals. He failed to notice. We did a few more moves and we got blasted again.

"Be in control but not at the expense of being literal!"

Again, he was referencing our very trained and upright posture. He wanted to see more—but not too much more—because he had a problem with too much as well.

"I want to see the step nude and pure. I want to see the anatomy of the chicken—meat and bones without the ruffles and feathers!"

He never took us aside to make us understand the corrections. He just shouted poetic phrases and moved on. I began to wonder if he liked shouting more than teaching. I felt like one of those Weeble Wobble toys instead of a New York City Ballet dancer.

After a week of three-hour rehearsals with him, all the dancers were feeling the tension. We were dancing on eggshells and feeling awkward, especially when he barked at one of the 16-year-olds.

"Get into it more! Let yourself go, damn it! It's like you're kissing with your damn eyes open!"

The comment wasn't necessary, but it didn't matter: we were ballet dancers and that meant keeping our mouths closed and following instructions. Everyone continued dancing, even though the 16-year-old was wallowing in tears. Eliot moved on with a new movement which—*God help me*—included me and one other girl. The step he gave was to move right to left in a zig zag pattern. He showed the step as having eight counts in each direction. We tried working the step out without music and all was fine, but when we tried it with music, it was muddled disarray.

"Try it again," he said, biting the air.

We tried again and I crashed into my partner because she kept moving when I stopped. I then realized that the music was 15 counts total, an eight and a seven. When he had first shown us the movement, he'd done it as 16, as if it were even. I was too afraid to speak up and figured I could just rig it somehow.

"What's going on? C'mon, again!"

It didn't work again, obviously, and this time he wasn't going to chance it yet again. "McBrearty!"

I was jolted. Why was it my fault? I guess I saw it coming ever since the first hour of tantrums, and now we were ending the second hour. I knew it was going to be bad when he didn't refer to me as Durbin or at least my first name, but he made no mistake in letting everyone know who he was talking to, and emphasized "McBrearty." Just like when your parents have their fill of you and they emphasize your first, middle, and last names—you know you are getting sent straight to bed. Except I wasn't six, I was 27, and I hadn't put bubble gum on my bed post: I'd simply gotten confused by the mismatch of his 16-count step with the 15-count music.

"Do you know the difference between the sane and the insane?" he quizzically fired in my direction.

Well, I thought, *those two words might describe me and you respectfully, but go on, I'm curious of your version.* Naturally I didn't respond, as he really wasn't expecting me to, and so he continued to answer his own question.

"The sane know that every time they make the same mistake, they get the same result! The insane think that making the same mistake will get them a different result!"

I knew my brow was half-wrinkled in wonder and half in disbelief of his approach to getting his point across. I could stand there being humiliated, or find the strength to speak up. Since our ballet master had been overlooking rehearsal and remained silent in the corner, I came to my own rescue.

"Well you see," I said. "I was doing the step in 16 like you asked, but I'm hearing a 15 in the music."

Tick…Tick…BOOM! With those words, I seemed to cultivate all of the world's electricity and centered it on his fury.

"Oh, McBrearty thinks she can tell me how it's done. Well, McBrearty, this is how it's done: STEP ASIDE!"

That was it. He looked at me like I was a she-devil daring to contradict him. One would have thought I had just stolen a lollipop from a child. One lousy count off the music, plus one lousy mood, equals one lousy moment. I was booted and replaced by an apprentice. *Thanks for the respect, Eliot, I'll make sure to return the favor.*

There was one hour left to the rehearsal and I was forced to sit on the floor and understudy while the rest of the dancers tiptoed around the steps as if they were holding a precious dodo bird, afraid to make any wrong moves that might prove to be detrimental. If he was trying to get the most out of his dancers, it seemed to me to be working the opposite effect.

Once the rehearsal was finished, I spoke with the ballet master. He tried convincing me that I needed to remain present at all the future rehearsals in order to be an example for the apprentices on how to be professional, even when someone else isn't, and that I may need to fill in if anyone got injured. I had spoken up in rehearsal, so I decided I may as well speak up for myself again. I did so in one statement: "I am not here to be a safety net. I am here to focus on my own improvement and artistry. I don't want to put myself back into a negative environment that will only infect my performance."

I really hated feeling like my ambitions were just simmering in a pot, which is what they would be doing if I were to remain sitting on the floor to the choreographer's amusement. Our ballet master understood and excused me. Even though the end result of avoiding the rehearsals altogether was the best possible scenario for me, I felt a tinge of sadness. I was disappointed in the experience with Eliot, and I was upset that the ballet master was willing to sacrifice my self-esteem by letting the lion use me as a "safety net." I realized then how easy it is to be taken advantage of if you are a ballerina without a voice. It was a learning experience.

Thinking back, it wasn't the only time I had to talk myself out of a potentially draining situation. Just a year prior I'd come down with mono. While recuperating, I had to miss rehearsal period and half the season. I wasn't sure what was wrong with me until the doctor called me one week into my feeling sick to tell me it was mono and highly contagious. I called one of my dancer friends two days later after she arrived back from a vacation in California. I had been on this trip with her and another dancer, but had flown home prior to my friends because I had been feeling sick. When I finally had the chance to tell her I had mono, she reacted as if I had been holding back evidence in a murder investigation.

"I was just visiting my grandmother and I shared my sandwich with her! If you passed this mono thing onto me while we were hanging out in California and let me share my food with my grandma and she dies because she gets mono, then you are sick!"

I thought I was doing the right thing by telling my friend as soon as she was back in town, but apparently she preferred to accuse me of calculated potential murder. She then got my other good friend who had been in California with us to gang up on me. I phoned that friend and was told, "You care more about dancing than you do your friends. We both know you were holding out on telling us about the mono thing so that the company wouldn't find out and you wouldn't lose your parts to us."

I was beginning to think my 105-degree fever was causing hallucinations of these warped conversations but no, they were real. I knew I was dealing with artists and artists come with drama, but this was Maury Povich-worthy. I tried apologizing—for what, I don't even know—but I only got drenched with more blame game negativity from them. I eventually resorted to allowing them to walk away from the friendship. If they could misconstrue and have such a warped vision of our friendship, then it was their choice and not mine.

The situation would drain me more than it would fulfill me, so I chose to walk away. It was difficult to get over, losing two friends that I had blindly seen as genuine. I also saw how easily one person's opinion can shape another's. The only comfort I found was in turning that loss into creativity. I wrote a poem that took an internal hurt and

turned it into an external situation. Despite the little strength
I had, I put myself to work for my own peace of mind.

Poem written in my journal:
Follow the Leader

You cannot know
I do not tell
I say everything's fine
You say you can't be well
You feel my silent presence is disturbing
I say look again at who is hurting
I hold more strength than I allow your eyes
To selectively perceive and monopolize
You cannot know
I do not tell
I need to guide myself
You need to cast a spell
We all want to play follow the leader
With our world at the head of the table
But we all follow the follower
Handle with care is our weak label
Goodbye to your ink blot staining,
Your magically delicious thoughts,
And superhero training
I choose to lead myself
I choose to follow my dream
Instead of living out a fable
Topped with cherries and cream
I observe, I watch you refuse to wake up
You try to sip the royal answers
From the wine in your cup
You struggle
As you strategically juggle

Your ideals in the board game of life
You try and occupy yourself singing castle songs
Pretending to lead a king's life
May I remind you
No matter how much you prearrange
It's those Promised Land endings
That are always subject to change.

We all have to remember that healing happens from within and creativity can be a salvation.

SPOTLIGHT LESSON

It's important in any industry you are in to build upon relationships. Knowing your own goals and personality well enough to stand up for yourself can help you navigate personalities different from your own by fitting the various facets together like puzzle pieces.

1. **Know that you're not the only one in the room.**
   Dancers don't commonly have a voice or opportunity to speak up since their bodies are their instruments. But if a choreographer or friend oversteps, feel free to stand up for yourself in a non-confrontational way.

2. **Take criticism well, if it's constructive.**
   Sometimes you may disagree with direction you are given, and it's not always behooving to speak up against it. In those cases, the artist you are working with may be extra meticulous or quirky, so take the direction with a grain of salt and weigh how it might be constructive advice to build upon rather than taking it personally.

Notes:

FULLY ENGAGE YOURSELF

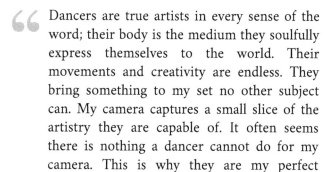

"Dancers are true artists in every sense of the word; their body is the medium they soulfully express themselves to the world. Their movements and creativity are endless. They bring something to my set no other subject can. My camera captures a small slice of the artistry they are capable of. It often seems there is nothing a dancer cannot do for my camera. This is why they are my perfect muses."
   - Steve Vaccariello

Often the company is referred to as one big happy family—which is true...sometimes. We spent so much of our existence together that we tended to know each other's moods and mannerisms inside and out. Only an environment that is so physically and mentally tuned-in and focused can bring such intimacy.

   We could identify one another by one's phrasing and musicality, wit and playfulness, understated confidence or natural assertion. Recognition came even with one's abandoned, broken-in pointe shoe sitting in the lost and found box backstage. We began to weld together in a way that only a family would, feeding off of each other. We began to rely on one another's artistic characteristics for further inspiration of our own. We leaned on one another—we were all in it together.

This attachment and comfort through familiarity was one element to our development and progress, but another deeper element was the audience. The performance wouldn't "be" without the dancers, but the dancers wouldn't "be" without the audience. For as long and strenuous as it was to prepare for a show, time was not sustained in the performance. It was fleeting, much too fleeting for our sacrifices to be acknowledged. This we didn't dwell on, but perhaps what we did dwell on was how to sustain our craft. The audience was how we were sustained, how we were recognized. The audience was what justified our existence. If it weren't for them, we couldn't have proven that fantasy existed in reality for a brief moment.

You see, a dancer's true existence is on stage. Their moments of purity and abandon are in performance and once witnessed by others, they live on in memory of all present. Frozen in time in the minds of our audience, yet carried through time by those same minds.

One evening after a performance, while I quietly sat in my apartment over a bowl of spaghetti, it became clear to me: unless the audience could fully see what our story was on the inside, the story on the outside couldn't be as rich. It was up to the dancer to translate her story. Unless the audience allows themselves to look deeper than the surface, they are missing the substance, and they go home with only the illusion—it is up to the audience to see the dancer's story.

I wrote a journal poem that night as an expression of this thought:

A Dancer's Story

The transformation from faulty mortal to delicate creature relies on the dancer's control over the audience's imagination.
Her body exists as the central instrument for language between them.
The dancer must convince every muscle and every limb to be strong and alert like the wind, yet fragile and soft in appearance like a feather.
It is important that she believe in her own story before attempting to invite the audience.
As the performance begins, gradually the audience and the stage lights fade together and away, leaving just the dancer and her story—one in which she has lived over and over in her thoughts before even beginning to physically convey.
Her body is a bird and her emotions human.
Her arms wildly flap, maintaining the appearance of rippling water.
Her tiny frame commands the wide stage of which is her sky as she soars into the shielding embrace of her prince.
The music, drawing closer, catches up with her flight and she now takes a pause in his presence.
With her movements much slower than her heartbeat, she is aware of every fiber working to create the illusion of effortlessness.
She engages herself in the fantasy and finds this to be the moment at which she accomplishes something beyond her own imagination.

Her balance is steady.

Her leaps mount high.

Her fast foot work is ready to allow her wings to fly.

There is magic in the inspiration that convinces her fears, and passion in her motion that moves the audience to tears.

The curtain comes down and for all tickets sold, she lived like a swan and her story was told.

———

I sat at the outdoor tables of Ernie's on Columbus Avenue with another dancer friend. We spoke about ballet, of course. She and I talked in rhythm, nourishing each other's arguments and opinions as to why we dance.

One reason was that sometimes we recaptured the 12-year-old's joy of inhibitions and fantasies that we wish we could indulge in more. Other times, we were aware of the moments in which we preferred not to speak, but rather were compelled to use body language and submit to our creative juices. Often times we lost sight of the "us" and danced solely to please Peter.

As we continued in our contemplation of drive and reason, two oversized boxes of Godiva chocolates—sealed and wrapped with a big red bow—were placed directly in front of us on our table. We looked up to see a total stranger. He was dressed in a very nice suit, but seemed to disappear as smoothly as the chocolates seemed to appear out of the air above. We promptly cranked our heads in his hurried direction.

From down the sidewalk, he called out: "I know the two of you are New York City Ballet and I am an admiring audience member. Accept these chocolates as my thank you for your work and dedication and know it is appreciated amongst us."

My friend and I were speechless. He could not have known the topic of our conversation for the last half hour. The irony and timing was impeccable, as if to remind us that whatever our drive was to dance, our art was what inspired others. I whipped my head back around to face my friend as we stared wide-eyed at each other, and then at the chocolates, and then AGAIN at the chocolates.

"This," I said, "is the force behind why I dance!"

"For chocolates?"

"No, the audience!"

Receiving acknowledgment from the inspired was what drove me to continue. It becomes a circle. We gave all of ourselves and another received. They received not what we are giving, but rather the inspiration that evaporates from what we give, and in turn they are compelled to give back. And so they did with the slightest acknowledgement of recognition that something was shared. This created the addiction to give and to get, to give more and to get more.

Journal entry:

Thirty-five long stem roses were left at the backstage entrance from a "Mr. Tengo."
The attached note read:
One for each of the lovely corps women who hold this company together.
Your biggest fan,
Mr. Tengo

Now I write to you, Mr. Tengo:
Thank you for your gentle support. In not even revealing your true

*identity as you thanked us, you displayed your selfless nature. You
deserve to be identified but even without It, we dance for you every
night and for others like you.*
With Gratitude,
Deanna

SPOTLIGHT LESSON

Do you have a story to tell? Are you willing to sacrifice to
tell it? How can you best convey it?

1. **Be so passionate that you transcend.** You must
   first believe in the story you are telling.
2. **Commit without inhibitions.** Combine your
   fears and passions so you forget about yourself and
   can begin portraying your story. Anything that
   really makes your heart beat wildly is worth
   conveying.

Notes:

SHARING ARTISTRY

 You should say 'Hi' to everyone, that's how you make friends."
- Cohen Parker, 7 years old

By remaining open-minded to the potential from where my inspiration could come, I was afforded opportunities in multiple arts disciplines throughout my career as a ballerina. I pushed myself and stayed open to trying new and creative experiences, which helped me grow as an artist, while sharing my art across multiple platforms.

ADVENTURE 1

One opportunity arose when one of the premier painter and sculpture artists in the world came to visit School of American Ballet. His name was George Carlson. He asked for four students willing to individually pose for him in a nearby Lincoln Center apartment, while he artistically captured the frozen dance movement into a sculpture of clay.

After weeks of standing still in a beam of natural light for hours at time, I was transformed into George Carlson's world where his eyes, hands, and all his other senses captured everything of meaning in a simple pose. I was also able to connect on a personal level while intermittently taking a break from posing long enough to chat and sip a mixture of Cranberry juice and seltzer along with a cup of Borsht soup homemade by his amazing wife Pam.

After a few months, the clay sculptures traveled back to Idaho with George to be made into bronzes for a series on ballet. Playing a role in his creative process was a humbling journey of artistic collaboration. He admired the delicate grace of a ballerina, and I admired his deep observation of life and his ability to translate it into art. He and his wife Pam are forever an inspiration to me as friends and artists.

Posing hours at a time for sculptor artist George Carlson in a sunny studio apartment near Lincoln Center, NYC.

ADVENTURE 2

NYCB typically toured Europe every summer, except for July 1999. We would have been out of work for the summer, but coincidentally Columbia Pictures was holding auditions for a new dance movie temporarily titled "The Dance Movie." Almost all of NYCB and ABT dancers auditioned, and a handful were chosen to be part of the film that was eventually titled, "Center Stage." Below is one account of this experience through my journal entries.

DAY 1, JULY 26

I learned what Craft Services means: Krispy Kremes all day! The 8 a.m. to 7p.m. day was filled with rehearsals, donuts, costume fittings…and more donuts.

DAY 2, JULY 27

Rehearsal was 9:30 a.m. -2:30 p.m. Susan Stroman works us hard! No mistakes allowed. All must be precise because it will be filmed and not a live show. Her assistant, Warren Carlyle, is awesome too. He dances the moves full out until we know it. He is also guilty of starting a fashion trend of wearing his pants pockets inside out. MTV came to film a short section for the *Jamiroquai* video.

DAY 4, JULY 29

Got make-up done professionally with glitter lips and slicked back buns to rehearse the scene with Michael Jackson's song, "The Way You Make Me Feel."

Filmed backstage chatter after performance and met the actress Donna Murphy, and the actor Peter Gallagher.

Found out from casting that I am being cast as Maureen's body double. I will film all of Susan May Pratt's scenes that require dance moves.

- **6:30 a.m.** Warm-up class taught by Jock Soto
- **9:30 a.m. - 3 p.m.** Filmed all of Christopher Wheeldon's choreography. The diagonal was

difficult for spacing, timing, and camera angle. After take 7, Nicholas Hytner, the director, noticed Zoe Saldana doesn't have her pearl earrings in that she was wearing in the first half of the footage! Oh no! Well, three more takes until we finally get another good one and Laura's pointe shoe ribbon came undone, making that take unusable. We did 12 takes of the diagonal until we had a perfect take where we were all traveling to our specific marks and staying together musically and no wardrobe malfunctions.

- **4 a.m. - 7:15 p.m.** Filmed Susan's 1st section scene with Michael Jackson song and wearing a white tutu. Ethan Stiefel did a few takes on a motorcycle. Sascha Radetsky acted as our teacher for the scene and helped us through. The crew has their own lingo for quick in-between needs: "Last Look" for make-up retouches. "Flashing" for polaroid shots for continuity. "Evian" if we all need to get sprayed with Evian water to look sweaty, again for continuity.

Some nights we filmed until 3am but it was all worth it to be part of such a fun film that helped ballet become mainstream again.

Sporting lobster bibs and sipping Starbucks in order to regain energy in between takes filming "Center Stage" at David H. Koch Theater. Pictured left to right: Aesha Ash, me and Riolama Lorenzo.

Having fun in between takes on movie set in Brooklyn, NY. Columbia Pictures' "Center Stage." Pictured with me: Natalia Haigler and Pascale Van Kipnis.

ADVENTURE 3

Working with renowned photographers at different times in my dance career always inspired me to recreate myself as an artist: to mash together their unique perspectives with my dance expression to build new ideas.

Richard Corman is a portrait photographer that truly knows how to capture spirit. He and I worked together on the *NYC Ballet Workout* book, as well as additional photo shoots for side projects of his.

I'll never forget our photoshoot at Chelsea Market in the dead of winter, with two feet of snow on the ground and golf ball-sized snowflakes trying to keep me from arriving at his fashion shoot for the 5 a.m. call. That day brought a flurry of action inside and out! Richard's humility and passion profoundly influenced me both artistically and personally.

My headshot taken by Richard Corman. Featured in both the "New York City Ballet Workout" book and in "Glory," Corman's book of athlete's photographs.

Bert Stern, famous for shooting *The Last Sitting* of Marilyn Monroe and Liz Taylor on the movie set of Cleopatra, photographed me for a Reebok ad campaign. I showed up in a tutu and a new pair of Reebok sneakers. He sat near a window for a photo shoot with me that would use only the day's natural light. He asked me to strike any dance pose that would show the sneakers well and would be a classic move for the campaign's title "Classical Classic."

A Reebok ad campaign entitled "Classic" conceived by Hegarty and BBH
U.S. It was an honor working with renowned photographer Bert Stern.

Rodney Smith is a famed photographer who, in my opinion, created dreams within his photos. He was commissioned by New York City Ballet to shoot our ad campaign. Two other dancers and I arrived at the top of the Chrysler Building, early in the morning for a photo shoot in the grand ballroom. It had been closed to the public for years, not experiencing the action it likely saw at the end of the Prohibition era. With three-inch layers of dust on the floor and window sills, it was a breathtaking, mystical day.

Photograph by Rodney Smith for New York City Ballet ad campaign. What an amazing time dancing for Rodney in the dust covered, grand ballroom, abandoned since prohibition, at the top of the Chrysler Building!

I was later invited by Rodney Smith to photo shoots at his home and nearby gardens so we could delve more into photographs with a whimsical purpose, as he was noted for.

A photo shoot for New York City Ballet ad campaign by photographer, Rodney Smith, featuring myself and Eva Natanya outside with dry ice affect in Symphony in C tutus. Photo credit Lydia Harmsen.

Jeffrey Milstein, a highly-awarded photographer, purchased an autographed pair of my worn pointe shoes from the gift shop while attending a performance at New York City Ballet. After the performance, he requested from security if he might be able to meet me. I came downstairs to security from my dressing room and greeted the photographer, who expressed interest in photographing the dancer that belonged to the autographed shoes.

He explained that he was President of Paper House Productions, a greeting card company, and asked if I would like to do a photo shoot with him in the School of American Ballet studios to print on a line of greeting cards. And so we did. Funny to think we met because of a shabby pair of threadbare shoes that were my trash, but to his artistic eye, they were a symbol of effort and endurance, thus his treasure.

A copy of the greeting card made by photographer Jeffrey Milstein using my "dead" pointe shoes.

Andrew Eccles and Jack Deutsch, two of the best photographers in the industry, were hired by Geoffrey Beene to shoot our sessions together. What fun I had combining crafts of dance, photography, fashion, and makeup! Andrew Eccles invited me to his studio one day and graciously handed me a compilation of our work together, creating my first professional portfolio. I treasure it still.

Me leaping for joy to work with photographer Andrew Eccles for Geoffrey Beene.

Paul Kolnik, a longtime New York City Ballet photographer, shot all of my on-stage performance photos. We also collaborated on the "NYCB Ballet Workout" DVD. I am grateful for his artistry and friendship that always encouraged me.

Some of the lovely crew associated with the filming of the first "New York City Ballet Workout" video.

Steve Vaccariello is a portrait, celebrity, and commercial photographer. Funny story—I did a photo shoot for a magazine spread that Steve Vaccariello happened to see. He immediately tracked me down by phone. He said he could shoot dance much better than that so we should collaborate on a project. That moment birthed our friendship and we have had many shoots together since that phone call!

Reaching new heights with Craig Hall. Bethesda Terrace and Fountain in New York's Central Park. Photo credit Steve Vaccariello.

Ira Lerner began his career as a photographer for *National Geographic* and later established himself as a top fashion and lifestyle photographer. We developed a long-lasting friendship from our work together and our mutual respect for each other's art.

Photographer Ira Lerner. Congress Park, downtown Saratoga Springs, NY

SPOTLIGHT LESSON:

When you put your best out there, other opportunities will arise. Take advantage of them. You will have new adventures and create a broadened network of friends.

1. **Be ready, willing, and able to show up for an adventure.** Enthusiasm is contagious.
2. **Appreciate the skills of others.** As an artist, there is always more to learn.

Notes:

AFTERWORD

Finding your identity through your craft means you gave yourself a voice! You have increased your chances of success by keeping a positive perspective. We can make a bigger impact when we are grounded in who we are as a person and as an artist.

So I want to thank you so much for reading *Start With This*. I hope you found it insightful and helpful. I would love to think that I was able to pass down my stories of experience to influence others to believe in themselves in the storms and have some affirming tools to send you leaping towards and beyond your dreams.

www.deannamcbrearty.com

PHOTOS

Me in the role of 5 girls for Balanchine's ballet, "Who Cares?" SAB workshop performance.

A view from the wings of me in Balanchine's "Bugaku."
Photograph taken by Christopher Wheeldon. New York City
Ballet. David H. Koch Theater.

Fancy Free
Music by Leonard Bernstein
Choreography by Jerome Robbins
Scenery by Oliver Smith

Costumes by Kermit Love
Lighting by Ronald Bates

Dancers (from left)
Damian Woetzel
Christopher Wheeldon
Deanna McBrearty
Tom Gold

New York City Ballet
Credit Photo:
© Paul Kolnik
Photo File No. C13565-7

Jerome Robbins' "Fancy Free," an amazingly fun and animated ballet. One of my favorites to dance with Christopher Wheeldon, Tom Gold, and Damian Woetzel. New York City Ballet. Photo credit Paul Kolnik.

Dancing my dream role of Maria with Benjamin Millepied in Jerome
Robbins' "West Side Story Suite." New York City Ballet. Photo credit Paul
Kolnik.

I would meet lots of celebrities backstage when they would attend a performance. Meeting THE Barbara Streisand was a highlight! From left to right: Paulin Golbin, Barbara Streisand, and me, after performing George Balanchine's "Vienna Waltzes." New York City Ballet. David H. Koch Theater.

Backstage at David H. Koch Theater after we filmed "You're Invited to Mary Kate and Ashley's Dance Party."

Meeting at the time Mayor Rudy Giuliani backstage after performing in Waltz of the Flowers, George Balanchine's "The Nutcracker." New York City Ballet.

New York City Ballet dancers after taping a 'Top Ten' sequence for "Late Night with David Letterman."

Me and the ever funny Hollywood star actor, John Lithgow, after performing together in the premier of Christopher Wheeldon's "Carnival of the Animals." Narration written by John Lithgow. New York City Ballet, David H. Koch Theater.

Performing demi-soloist role in Peter Martins' ballet, "Ash." Pictured with me are Stephen Hanna and James Fayette. New York City Ballet, David H. Koch Theater. Photo credit Daniel C. Casaglia.

A serene moment between me and Christopher Wheeldon captured by photographer Paul Kolnik. New York City Ballet Workout.

The cover of my own workout video, "Balocity." Photo credit Sean Murray and Christopher Ewers.

A visit to Bertram Mandell's home in Arizona. I am forever grateful to this gracious man that gave me my scholarship to School of American Ballet.

Love and Cheers to my family for all your support.

I love you, you're in my heart.

ABOUT THE AUTHOR

Deanna Mcbrearty was an exceedingly accomplished dancer with New York City Ballet from 1992 to 2004, dancing numerous featured and principal roles and working with renowned choreographers such as Jerome Robbins, Peter Martins, Susan Stroman, Christopher Wheeldon, Twyla Tharp, and more. During her years at NYCB and beyond, Deanna has been one of the most active and entrepreneurial members of that company. Her television credits include America's Health Network, O Network, and FOX-TV, as well as "The David Letterman Show."

Deanna has also appeared in films, including Columbia Pictures' *Center Stage*. She forged a career in media and fitness instruction with credits that include major television networks and workout DVDs. She has been the spokesmodel for Danskin Dancewear Inc. and Just For Kix dance apparel, as well as a featured fashion model for Geoffrey Beene for 12 years, including gracing two covers of books on his work.

She has choreographed two children's Dance-A-Long videos (*Barbie in the 12 Dancing Princesses* and *Barbie in the Island Princess*) in collaboration with Mattel Entertainment Inc. She is also co-founder and creator of a dance inspired workout DVD entitled "Balocity" – named a Top 10 Dance-Inspired Workout by *Prevention Magazine*.

Deanna has also provided fitness training to celebrities such as Kelly Ripa, Christy Turlington, Natasha Lyonne, and Maura Tierny, among others. She has also written for many leading dance publications including *Pointe Magazine, Dance Spirit,* and *Dance Magazine.*

Deanna currently mentors young women in the pursuit of professional dance careers and teaches pre-pro ballet level students. She lives in the Charleston area where she is raising her two children along with her husband, Steve Parker Jr.

instagram.com/deannamcbrearty

31347901R00091

Made in the USA
Middletown, DE
30 December 2018